BIBLIOGRAPHY OF CRITICISM
ON ENGLISH AND FRENCH
LITERARY TRANSLATIONS
IN CANADA

BIBLIOGRAPHIE DE LA CRITIQUE
DES TRADUCTIONS LITTÉRAIRES
ANGLAISES ET FRANÇAISES
AU CANADA

BIBLIOGRAPHY OF CRITICISM ON ENGLISH AND FRENCH LITERARY TRANSLATIONS IN CANADA

1950-1986
ANNOTATED

KATHY MEZEI

With the assistance of Patricia Matson and Maureen Hole

**University of Ottawa Press /
Canadian Federation for the Humanities**

*cahiers de traduc**T**ologie*

$\dfrac{}{7}$

BIBLIOGRAPHIE DE LA CRITIQUE DES TRADUCTIONS LITTÉRAIRES ANGLAISES ET FRANÇAISES AU CANADA

DE 1950 À 1986
AVEC COMMENTAIRES

KATHY MEZEI

Avec la collaboration de Patricia Matson et Maureen Hole

Les Presses de l'Université d'Ottawa /
Fédération canadienne des études humaines

© University of Ottawa Press, 1988
ISBN 0-7766-0198-9
Printed and bound in Canada

Canadian Cataloguing in Publication Data

Mezei, Kathy, 1947-
Bibliography of criticism on English and French
literary translations in Canada : 1950-1986 =
Bibliographie de la critique des traductions
littéraires anglaises et françaises au Canada de
1950-1986

(Translation studies = Cahiers de traductologie ; 7)
Text in English and French.   Includes indexes.
ISBN 0-7766-0198-9

1. Canadian literature (English)—Translations into
French—History and criticism—Bibliography.
2. Canadian literature (French)—Translations
into English—History and criticism—Bibliography.
3. Translations—History and criticism—Bibliography.
I. Hole, Maureen   II. Matson, Patricia   III. Title.
IV. Title: Bibliographie de la critique des traductions
littéraires anglaises et françaises au Canada de
1950 à 1986. V. Series: Cahiers de traductologie ; 7.

Z1377.T7M49 1988   016.81′09   C88-090194-2E

Données de catalogage avant publication (Canada)

Mezei, Kathy, 1947-
Bibliography of criticism on English and French
literary translations in Canada : 1950-1986 =
Bibliographie de la critique des traductions
littéraires anglaises et françaises au Canada de
1950-1986

(Translation studies = Cahiers de traductologie ; 7)
Texte en anglais et en français.   Comprend des index.
ISBN 0-7766-0198-9

1. Littérature canadienne-anglaise—Traductions
françaises—Histoire et critique—Bibliographie.
2. Littérature canadienne-française—Traductions
anglaises—Histoire et critique—Bibliographie.
3. Traductions—Histoire et critique—Bibliographie.
I. Hole, Maureen   II. Matson, Patricia   III. Titre.
IV. Titre: Bibliographie de la critique des traductions
littéraires anglaises et françaises au Canada de
1950 à 1986. V. Collection: Cahiers de traductologie ; 7.

Z1377.T7M49 1988   016.81′09   C88-090194-2F

This book has been published with the help of a grant from the Canadian Federation for the Humanities, using funds provided by the Social Sciences and Humanities Research Council of Canada.

Cet ouvrage a été publié grâce à une subvention de la Fédération canadienne des études humaines, dont les fonds proviennent du Conseil de recherches en sciences humaines du Canada.

Table of Contents
Table des matières

Preface

In co-publishing Professor Mezei's bibliography with the University of Ottawa Press, the Canadian Federation for the Humanities commemorates more than two decades of active involvement with scholarly translation in Canada.

From its earliest days as the Humanities Research Council of Canada, founded in 1943, the Federation supported research projects, symposia, surveys of the humanities, and scholarly publications in both French and English. When most of its funding programmes were handed over to the newly created Canada Council in 1957, CFH retained its Aid to Scholarly Publications Programme, which it continues to administer with its sister federation in the social sciences. By the late 1960s the number of significant academic books existing only in English or in French became a matter of concern, and the CFH Committee on Translation was formed in 1970.

The committee's first work was to approach the Secretary of State of Canada and the Canada Council to urge the creation of a programme of aid for translation, which was finally announced in 1972. The committee then undertook new functions: to recommend to the Canada Council appropriate scholarly titles for cross-translation, and to prepare inventories of qualified translators and assessors. Its work expanded to include history, philosophy, religious studies, linguistics, music, and both literatures. The Federation sponsored a research project for the committee, which resulted in the pioneering bibliography by Stratford and Newman in 1975, listed here as item 169. A much expanded second edition was also published by CFH two years later.

Since then the committee's membership has grown to include translators and publishers working in both languages. Research for a comprehensive bibliography of translated books is under way, and the Federation continues to press for an independent programme to aid the translation and publication of scholarly works. It is with understandable pleasure, then, that the Federation is associated with the publication of Professor Mezei's bibliography.

Viviane F. Launay, Executive Director
Canadian Federation for the Humanities

Ottawa, April 1988

Préface

En co-publiant la bibliographie de madame Mezei avec les Presses de l'Université d'Ottawa, la Fédération canadienne des études humaines célèbre plus de deux décennies d'activités dans le domaine de la traduction savante au Canada.

Dès sa fondation en 1943 en tant que Conseil canadien de recherches sur les humanités, la Fédération a financé des projets de recherches, des colloques, des enquêtes sur l'état de la discipline, et des ouvrages savants écrits en français ou en anglais. Lorsqu'en 1957 le Conseil des arts du Canada a commencé à administrer les programmes de recherches, la FCEH a continué d'être responsable du Programme d'aide à l'édition savante, qu'elle administre toujours conjointement avec sa fédération-sœur en sciences sociales. À la fin des années soixante, la Fédération s'inquiéta du nombre grandissant d'ouvrages scientifiques marquants qui n'étaient disponibles qu'en français ou en anglais ; c'est ainsi que le Comité de traduction de la FCEH vit le jour en 1970.

Le Comité commença son travail en exerçant des pressions auprès du Secrétariat d'État et du Conseil des arts pour que soit créé un programme d'aide à la traduction, qui fut établi en 1972. Puis le Comité diversifia ses tâches en recommandant au Conseil des arts une liste d'ouvrages qui devraient être disponibles dans nos deux langues officielles ; il prépara aussi un répertoire des traducteurs et des évaluateurs compétents. Les ouvrages suggérés portaient sur l'histoire, la philosophie, les études religieuses, la linguistique, la musique et nos deux littératures. La Fédération parraina également un projet de recherche qui donna naissance à la fameuse bibliographie de Stratford et Newman en 1975 : elle figure ici au numéro 169. Une seconde édition, considérablement augmentée, fut publiée par la FCEH deux ans plus tard.

Depuis lors, traducteurs et éditeurs se sont joints au Comité. La recherche pour mener à bien la publication d'une bibliographie exhaustive de tous les ouvrages traduits en français ou en anglais va bon train et la Fédération continue à promouvoir l'établissement d'un programme autonome d'aide à la traduction et à la publication d'ouvrages savants. C'est donc avec un immense plaisir que la Fédération s'associe à la publication de la bibliographie de madame Mezei.

Viviane F. Launay, Directeur général
Fédération canadienne des études humaines

Ottawa, avril 1988

Acknowledgements

This bibliography could not have been completed without the kind advice, suggestions, and assistance of the following colleagues: Harvey De Roo, Jean Delisle, Sandra Djwa, Ray Ellenwood, Carole Gerson, Richard Giguère, Barbara Godard, Percilla Groves, Paul Hjartarson, David Homel, Tünde Nemeth, Sherry Simon, Michael Steig, the Simon Fraser University Library Reference and Interlibrary Loans Division, and the Department of English at Simon Fraser University, particularly Honorée Newcombe, Lynn Hill, and Heather Coleman. I am very grateful to David Hayne for his careful reading of the manuscript.

For his patience and ingenuity in creating a computer programme, I thank Wolfgang Richter, Computing Centre, Simon Fraser University.

I acknowledge with much gratitude the generosity of the SSHRCC Canadian Studies Research Tools Programme, the SFU President's Research Grant, the SFU Publications Committee Grant, and the generosity of Bob Brown, Dean of Arts, for making this project possible.

For having encouraged my interest in literary translation, I warmly thank Sheila Fischman, Philip Stratford, D.G. Jones, Larry Shouldice, and Eva Mezei.

Even a bibliography on translation requires translation, and for their excellent contributions I thank Joëlle Da Cunha (annotations, indexes) and Réjean Beaudoin (introduction).

My special thanks to Bob Anderson for his support and good humour throughout this process.

And finally, for their cheerful, patient, and invaluable assistance, I thank my research assistants, Maureen Hole who courageously began the project, and Patricia Matson who took it over and, with great aplomb and skill, brought it to completion.

Remerciements

Cette bibliographie n'aurait pas pu être rassemblée sans l'aimable colla-
boration et les précieux conseils des collègues dont les noms suivent :
Harvey De Roo, Jean Delisle, Sandra Djwa, Ray Ellenwood, Carole Gerson,
Richard Giguère, Barbara Godard, Percilla Groves, Paul Hjartarson, David
Homel, Tünde Nemeth, Sherry Simon, Michael Steig, le personnel des
services de consultation et de prêt inter-bibliothèques de la bibliothèque de
Simon Fraser University ainsi que les membres du Département d'anglais
de cette même université, en particulier Honorée Newcombe, Lynn Hill et
Heather Coleman. Je suis très reconnaissante à David Hayne de sa lecture
attentive de mon manuscrit.

Pour sa patience et son ingéniosité à mettre au point un programme
informatique, je remercie Wolfgang Richter du Computing Centre, Simon
Fraser University.

J'exprime également mes plus sincères remerciements au personnel
de la section Études canadiennes : outils de recherche du CRSHC, au
President's Research Grant, au Publications Committee Grant, Simon Fraser
University, et au généreux doyen de la faculté des Arts, Bob Brown, qui
ont rendu possible la réalisation de ce projet.

Je remercie aussi chaleureusement Sheila Fischman, Philip Stratford,
D.G. Jones, Larry Shouldice et Eva Mezei qui ont nourri mon intérêt pour
la traduction littéraire.

Puisque même une bibliographie sur la traduction comporte un
certain travail de traduction, je remercie Joëlle Da Cunha (annotations,
index) et Réjean Beaudoin (introduction) de leur excellente contribution à
mon ouvrage.

Enfin, pour leur aide empressée et leur patience inestimable, j'exprime ma gratitude à mes assistantes de recherche, Maureen Hole, qui a
courageusement mis le projet en marche, et Patricia Matson, qui l'a relayée
pour le mener à terme avec beaucoup d'assurance et de dextérité.

Introduction

WHY THIS BIBLIOGRAPHY?

> As with medicine, literature and child psychology, everybody is an expert without even suspecting that there are things to be studied.[1]

> Les mots nous choisissent autant que nous les choisissons, surtout ceux d'une langue étrangère.[2]

This bibliography covers critical writing on literary translation in Canada in the two official languages from 1950 to 1986. Although much has been written on translation in Canada during this time, we have included only items that refer to the translation of Canadian literature in French and English. As the number of entries indicates, this area of literary translation studies[3] has gradually and surely developed into a significant field of criticism, embracing such diverse subjects as comparative literature, communications, linguistics, sociolinguistics, feminism, politics, and creative writing. As a discipline it is invariably promiscuous (despite some translators' claim of "fidelity"), polysystemic, metatextual. Appropriately, the art of literary translation and its theory and practice have attracted an eclectic range of practitioners from the dilettante to the academic scholar.

This bibliography will demonstrate not just that much material has been written about Canadian literary translation, but that its quality and variety are considerable. Yet there are still many "things to be studied," and the study of literary translation in this country remains in its early stages. What then is the rationale behind this bibliography?

First of all, such a bibliography is timely, for translation theory and translation studies are poised on a threshold, ready to be launched in earnest. As evidence, one has only to note the mounting number of conferences, panel discussions, publications, the national and international activities of the Association of Literary Translators/Association des traducteurs littéraires, and the formation of the Association canadienne de traductologie.

Second, the bibliography and annotations serve, on the one hand, as a historical document, overtly recording the extent and development of critical writing on the translation of Canadian literature in French and English, and covertly recording the history of modern literary translation in Canada. On the other hand, they also inevitably prepare the ground for future studies, which will mark lacunae and signal necessary new directions.

Third, as with any developing and slightly suspect field of study, material is frequently located in unexpected places. We hope therefore that our own detective work will facilitate the future efforts of researchers or of the simply curious.

And finally, the scope of this bibliography is both a consequence of and a testament to the flourishing of literary activity in the 60s and 70s, the enterprising and inspired translators who responded to this renaissance, and the subsequent dramatic increase in translations and accompanying critical apparatus in the form of reviews, articles, and interviews.

THE DEVELOPMENT AND EXTENT OF LITERARY TRANSLATION STUDIES
ON CANADIAN LITERATURE IN FRENCH AND ENGLISH

Translation

Translation has been an integral part of the political and intellectual life of Canada from as early as 1534. It was then that Jacques Cartier took two sons of the Iroquois chief, Donnacona, back with him to France, where they learned French; when they returned eight months later to the New World, they acted as interpreters at Stadacona (Quebec City) between the French and the Iroquois.[4] Translation was given official status by the language provisions of the BNA Act of 1867, and by 1934 a federal Bureau of Translation had been created. Commercial, technical, and government translation have become essential to the operation of Canadian society.

However, the necessity for translation, and the consequences, particularly for Quebec, of being a translated culture, create serious problems: the subordination of one language and cultural group to the more dominant one, the gradual but persistent infiltration and corruption of the subordinate language, and the subsequent effect on the cultural sovereignty and uniqueness and will of the subordinate culture.[5]

Literary translation

Unlike public translation, which has been a legislated necessity, literary translation has evolved in a more haphazard fashion. Writers, attracted by the challenge to their creativity and by the pleasure of being immersed in issues of style and language, have turned their hand to literary translation: Philippe Aubert de Gaspé, Charles G.D. Roberts, F.R. Scott, John Glassco, Fred Cogswell, D.G. Jones, Daphne Marlatt, Claire Martin, Jacques Brault, Michel Beaulieu. Authors and translators have entered into dialogues, with reverberations for both: Anne Hébert and F.R. Scott, Gabrielle Roy and Joyce Marshall, Roch Carrier and Sheila Fischman, Jacques Ferron with Ray Ellenwood and Betty Bednarski, Daphne Marlatt and Nicole Brossard.

With missionary zeal, some translators wish to convert their audience to the delights or virtues of a particular text or author in the other language. During the late 50s, 60s, and early 70s, when Quebec literature was undergoing its quiet revolution, and when Quebec independence seemed a possibility, translation activity, particularly from French to English, rapidly gained momentum.

Translators have also been motivated by the political and cultural role that literary translation plays. As F.R. Scott remarked in his Preface to *Poems of French Canada*, "translation is not only an art in itself, it is also an essential ingredient in Canada's political entity."[6] Over and over again, translators, authors, and commentators describe literary translation as a bridge between two solitudes, and translators see themselves as cultural mediators. Paradoxically, the need for translation and the quantity of translations are stark admission that the two solitudes exist. Moreover, the traffic over the imaginary bridge from English Canada is substantially less than that over the one leading from Quebec to English Canada. In his *Oxford Companion to Canadian Literature* article, "Translations: French to English,"[7] John O'Connor claims that as of 1983, 550 French to English but only 400 English to French literary texts had been translated. Less than 20% of the entries in this bibliography are in French, concretely demonstrating that Quebec has paid less attention to translations from the English.[8] As Jacques Brault commented in *Poèmes des quatre côtés*, "Nous n'aimons ni traduire ni être traduits: les clefs de la traduction appartiennent aux puissants."[9] A number of French and English critics have pointed out these disappointing statistics and suggested some tentative reasons.[10] While Quebec's deliberate insularity, its anxiety about English imperialism, and a preference for American over Canadian literature may account for some of these reasons, this subject deserves deeper study.

Although literary translation was a not insignificant aspect of nineteenth and early twentieth-century literary life,[11] and several major authors, especially Quebec authors—Gabrielle Roy, Roger Lemelin, Ringuet, Félix-Antoine Savard—were all translated in the 40s, after the Second World War, there was a gradual increase in translations, as well as in literary journals that would provide venues for both translations and reviews.

In 1960, P.F. Widdows published his translations of Émile Nelligan's *Selected Poems*,[12] while Jean Beaupré and Gael Turnbull had brought out their translations of Saint-Denys Garneau, Roland Giguère, Gilles Hénault, and Paul-Marie Lapointe in the Contact Press series during the 50s. F.R. Scott's translations of Saint-Denys Garneau first appeared in *The Tamarack Review* 4 (1957), and of the Quebec poets Pierre Trottier, Anne Hébert, Jean-Guy Pilon, Roland Giguère, and Gilles Hénault in *The Tamarack Review* 7 (1958); and *St. Denys Garneau and Anne Hébert* was published by Klanak Press in 1962.

The "nouveau roman," revolutionary in form and theme, which erupted upon the Quebec literary scene in the 60s, aroused the interest of English Canadians and invited translation; novels by Hubert Aquin, Gérard Bessette, Marie-Claire Blais, Jacques Godbout, Claude Jasmin, André Langevin, Jacques Renaud were translated, though relatively slowly, with three- or four-year gaps between source and target text. In contrast, only Stephen Leacock, Hugh MacLennan, and Margaret Laurence (and Mazo de la Roche) appeared in French versions during that time. Of dramatists in both languages, only Gratien Gélinas had been translated by 1969.

In 1972, translation activity had both increased in quantity and received official recognition and support with the inauguration of the Canada Council Translation Grant Programme. By 1973 the Canada Council Translation Prizes had been created, and two years later the Association of Literary Translators/Association des traducteurs littéraires was founded. Small English-Canadian presses, like Anansi, Oberon, Talonbooks, Coach House Press, along with the more established publishers, McClelland and Stewart and General Publishing, were prepared to publish translations, and in the case of the small presses translations of experimental texts. Harvest House, an English-language press in Montreal, which published Claude Jasmin's *Ethel and the Terrorist* (translated by David S. Walker in 1965), began putting out its "French Writers of Canada" series in earnest in the 70s. The first issue of *Ellipse*, a journal devoted to publishing work in translation, appeared in 1969, while John Glassco's ground-breaking anthology, *Poetry of French Canada in Translation*, was published in 1970, rapidly followed by Fred Cogswell's collections, *One Hundred Poems of Modern Quebec* (1970) and *A Second Hundred Poems of Modern Quebec* (1971).

In Quebec, Le Cercle du Livre de France began its "Collection des Deux Solitudes" in 1973, featuring Morley Callaghan, Robertson Davies, Margaret Laurence, Mordecai Richler, Brian Moore, W.O. Mitchell. Several writers—Leonard Cohen, Mordecai Richler, Audrey Thomas, Malcolm Lowry—had been published in France.

The first edition of Philip Stratford and Maureen Newman's indispensable *Bibliography of Canadian Books in Translation/Bibliographie de livres canadiens traduits* was published in 1975, an indication of the growing importance of literary translation.

In the 80s, certain significant changes have occurred. More Quebec publishers—Québec-Amérique, Éditions HMH, Fides, Héritage, L'Étincelle, Les Éditions Leméac—have entered the translation field; more contemporary poetry is being translated into English through enterprising presses—Guernica Editions, Véhicule Press, Coach House Press, Exile Editions; there has been an increase in translations (and productions) of plays, and a somewhat shorter gap exists between the publication of the source and target texts. Feminist texts from Quebec are starting to receive attention, with recent translations of Nicole Brossard, Louky Bersianik and Jovette Marchessault. Experiments in translation, such as *Ellipse 8x8* (29/30, 1982), in which four English and four French poets translated, in a series, a poem by each, or Daphne Marlatt and Nicole Brossard's intertexts or "transformations," *Mauve* and *Jeu de lettres/Characters*[13] signal a new stage in translation studies. Translators of difficult texts, Ray Ellenwood (the automatiste Claude Gauvreau), Barbara Godard (Nicole Brossard), Patricia Claxton (Nicole Brossard), preface their translations with descriptions of their translation process.[14]

Translation criticism
A diachronic survey of critical material becomes a history of attitudes towards bilingualism, towards the other solitude, and towards the art and act of literary translation.

Although certain journals in the late 50s and during the 60s (*The Tamarack Review, Prism International, Liberté*) were hospitable to translation and to reviews of translations, translation was regarded with some suspicion, and much space was devoted to justification. Reviewers were often unilingual, commenting on texts without acknowledging either the translator, or that they were translated from another language. I have come across one or two reviews stating that the translations were poor, even though the reviewer could not or had not read the original!

As our annotations reveal, certain predictable comments recur:
1. the difficulty of translating poetry
2. the difficulty of translating (especially from French to English) dialect, swear words, slang, and *joual*
3. whether the title was successfully rendered
4. whether the tone or spirit of the source text was "captured"
5. where the particular rendition rests on the sliding scale of free, faithful, or literal
6. the inclusion of a token example of mistranslation

By the late 60s and in the 70s, on the heels of the institutionalization of translation through the Canada Council and publishers' translation series, the critical apparatus surrounding translation matured. First of all, both translators and reviewers felt less compelled to justify their activities, and began to examine the processes involved. Many reviewers were bilingual, and could compare in depth the source and target text; many were translators themselves: Gwladys Downes, Philip Stratford, D.G. Jones were among those who wrote perceptive accounts of translated texts, foregoing plot summaries to provide readers with detailed assessments of the translation within a theoretical framework.

A persistent theme in critical commentary has been advocacy: arguing for institutional support, urging the need for more translations, claiming the importance of translation as a "bridge" between two cultures, and lamenting the lack of translations or of translations of important or classic source texts. Critics and translators have also repeatedly stressed the need for competent translations, and for retranslations—of Gabrielle Roy's *The Tin Flute* (by Hannah Josephson), Jean-Charles Harvey's *Sackcloth for Banner* (by Lukin Barette), and Jacques Renaud's *Flat, Broke and Beat* (by Gérald Robitaille).[15] It seems each generation must indeed retranslate for itself.

The noticeable shift towards metatranslation in the 80s, whereby discussions of the process of translation are incorporated either into or along with the published text, reflect changes in the status and focus of translation studies. Examples of metatranslation occur in Guernica's bilingual editions, the commentaries in the *Ellipse 8x8* issue, and more frequent translators' explanatory prefaces. Recently, different strategies have been undertaken. In response to postmodern and feminist texts, reviewers and critics have been forced to reexamine concepts such as literal translation (literal semantically or syntactically?) and the manifestation of sexual difference and gender in both source and target languages, and in the process of transfer from one to the other. Drawing on the question of context in translation studies, Ben-Zion Shek[16] and E.D. Blodgett[17] have pointed out the dangers inherent in translation in a country where diglossia exists. Philip Stratford, Patricia Claxton, and Ray Ellenwood[18] have discussed the often unsatisfactory history of literary translation, and analyzed the policies of the federal government.

From this perspective, therefore, we can see that translation studies has apparently divided into the following branches: history, culture and politics, literary criticism and comparative literature, practice, theory, adaptation and tradaptation,[19] and gender.[20]

It is the increase in what E.D. Blodgett would call "Canadian meditations," which can be found in the publication of discrete articles on literary translation in journals, the annual review of translations in *The University of Toronto Quarterly*, the symposium and proceedings, *Translation in Canadian Literature* (1983), and *La Traduction, l'universitaire et le praticien* (1984), that brings translation studies in Canada to the threshold. As this bibliography goes to press, the number of publications on translation in process are evidence of this take-off: future special issues of *Canadian Literature* [117] and *Translation Review* (Dallas); Jean Delisle's monumental history of translation, *La Traduction au Canada/Translation in Canada 1534-1984* (Ottawa: Les Presses de l'Université d'Ottawa, 1987); the forthcoming publication of the proceedings from the October 1986 Literary Translators' Association conference, "Literary Translation and Literary Identity," by Véhicule Press, and of the panel discussion on the relation between author and translator from the 1983 "Women and Words" conference in *Meta*; and special sessions on translation at the Malcolm Lowry conference in May 1987, and at the Canadian Comparative Literature Association sessions during the Learned Societies Meetings in 1986 and 1987. Since 1981, two new translation prizes have been inaugurated: the John Glassco Translation Prize and the F.R. Scott Translation Prize, in honour of two pioneers of literary translation.

SO WHAT REMAINS TO BE DONE?

While this bibliography indeed marks a threshold, it discloses, at the same time, a certain lack. What further developments are then indicated?

1. *Theory and terminology:* Although general translation theory[21] derived from comparative linguistics has been relatively well formulated, literary translation has been less so.[22] Similarly, as E.D. Blodgett points out, "Canadian meditations on translation are neither as plentiful nor as various as they might be."[23] Interestingly enough, 6 out of 37 M.A. theses that are translations do not include comments on the translation theory or practice of the translator in their introductions. Until now, theoretical approaches have focussed on

i. Discussion of the relative merits of free, literal, and faithful translation.

ii. D.G. Jones's concept of translation as "effective communion"[24]—a sophisticated version of translation as a bridge between two cultures.

iii. Jacques Brault's description of his practice as "nontraduction"[25]—*laisser-faire* applied creatively to the translation of poetry.

iv. Translation as polysystem and translation in the literary polysystem, which is E.D. Blodgett's adaptation to the Canadian context of Itamar Even-Zohar's concept of literature as a complex, dynamic "conglomerate of systems."[26]

Critics and reviewers need to construct, as Annie Brisset, E.D. Blodgett, and Sherry Simon are currently in the process of doing, workable theoretical models to analyze the complex set of interrelations that literary translation in Canada involves. "Faithful translation," "capture of tone," "does not do justice to the original" are tired expressions that reveal a poverty of analysis and do not adequately describe the leaps of imagination and complex operations of translators. We need to go beyond. Rather than merely enumerating mistranslations, critics should probe the nature and significance of these errors and lapses.

2. *Further studies of the political and cultural role of literary translation:* questions that need to be addressed are: i. who is translated (and who is not); ii. the role of institutions such as the Canada Council, publishing houses and their editors, the Association of Literary Translators, the journal *Ellipse* (who is translated, who are the translators, translating and editorial policies).

3. *Translation process:* the study of translators' practices in both decoding the source text and encoding it into the target text, of decisions concerning, for example, the treatment of English expressions in translating from the French source text, or the equivalent terms for regionalisms, swearing, *joual*. The role of translators' notes or prefaces is an important aspect of documenting the translation process. As Barbara Godard points out in her "Preface" to *Lovhers:* "One could write a history of theories of translation, a history of the relationships between author and translator, indeed between author and reader by writing a history of the preface as genre."[27] In other words, we need analysis of the translator as reader and writer.

4. *More histories of literary translation:* studies of literary translation in different historical periods, and of the history of a translated text or of different versions of a source text, for example, of *Maria Chapdelaine*.

5. *Further work:* on the applicability of polysystem theory, on the imprinting of sexual difference, on adaptation in theatre, on translation and intertextuality and metatextuality, on author-translator relations, and on translation as reading and interpretation.

NOTES TO THE USER

Scope and style of bibliography
This bibliography extends from 1950 to 1986, with the opening date of 1950 chosen because of the increase in literary translation after World War Two. The citation form is that of the *MLA Style Manual* (1985), which we followed in both French and English entries for consistency, with one exception: reviews of translations include full publication details—place,

publisher, and date—in order that the user have complete information at hand.

Annotations

The type of annotation is commentary (not paraphrase), and the approach is non-evaluative.

Categories

The categories, under which criticism on literary translation in Canada is organized, consist of: *articles, bibliographies, books, interviews, introductions* (includes all prefaces, forewords, afterwords, prefatory translator's notes, editor's introductions), *review articles, reviews* (includes only reviews that **evaluate** translations in some detail and in general provide examples), *theses, translators' notes* (extensive notes **within** the body of the translation).

We have not included material referring to children's literature, with the exception of the appendix.

Methodology

Items in this bibliography were selected according to their pertinence to the subject of literary translation in Canada; we have examined all the references listed.

All bibliographers operate through a combination of methodical investigation, intuition, and happenstance. A casual glance through a book on a library shelf may turn up a pertinent article. Microfiches and databases, however efficient and time-saving, cannot replace browsing through bookshelves and the pages of journals, or receiving helpful suggestions from colleagues.

Our sources include but are not limited to standard indexes: *Canadian Periodical Index; Canadian Essay and Literature Index; Radar; Périodex; Point de repère; Index Translationum; Canadian Book Review Annual; Canadian Literature Index*; and bibliographies: *MLA Bibliography; Bibliography of Canadian Books in Translation/Bibliographie de livres canadiens traduits* (1977); the Hayne-Sirois "Preliminary Bibliography of Comparative Canadian Literature" series; *International Bibliography of Translation: Index*; the "Annual Bibliography of Commonwealth Literature"; the "Canadian Literature/Littérature canadienne: an annotated bibliography/une bibliographie avec commentaire" series, edited by Bruce Nesbitt; the "Bibliographie" in the *Revue d'histoire littéraire du Québec et du Canada français*.

Index

Explanations and instructions to users about indexes are located at the beginning of each index. The user should also note that, although translation theory possesses an extensive terminology, very little of it appears in the index, simply because it was not used by the critics, and therefore did not occur in the material. The French subject index contains more translation terms, many drawn from Jean-Paul Vinay and Jean Darbelnet's *Stylistique comparée du français et de l'anglais* (Paris: Didier, 1958). Finally, I should like to draw the reader's attention to Wittgenstein's celebrated statement that "the meaning of a word is its use in the language," to the obvious fact that translation is concerned with language, and that naturally much of the criticism is language-oriented; therefore many headings in the subject index are related to language, although "language" itself is not a heading. The specifically language-related headings are: colloquialisms; English expressions, treatment of, in translating from French source text; English expressions, presence in French source text; dialect; errors, lexical; *faux amis*; French, different forms of; French, retention of in English translation; *joual*; linguistic competence; linguistic context; linguistic untranslatability; neologisms.

Cross-references

We direct the user to the indexes instead of to a cumbersome system of cross-references. Only articles referring to other articles or reviews in the bibliography are cross-referenced. Joint authors are also cross-referenced.

NOTES

1. Itamar Even-Zohar, "Translation Theory Today," *Poetics Today* 2.4 (1981): 1.
2. Jacques Brault, *Poèmes des quatre côtés* (Saint-Lambert: Éditions du Noroît, 1975) 14.
3. Susan Bassnet-McGuire, quoting André Lefevere's proposal, defines translation studies as "the discipline that concerns itself with problems raised by the production and description of translations." *Translation Studies* (London: Methuen, 1983) 1.
4. Jean Delisle, "Les Pionniers de l'interprétation au Canada," *Meta* 22.1 (mars 1977): 5-15.
5. See Pierre Chantefort, *Diglossie au Québec; limites et tendances actuelles* (Québec: Les Presses de l'Université Laval, 1970); Ben-Zion Shek, "Quelques réflexions sur la traduction dans le contexte socio-culturel canado-québécois," *Ellipse* 21 (1977): 111-117.
6. Burnaby: Blackfish Press, 1977, vi.

7. Toronto: Oxford, 1983, 795-796.
8. However, André Gagnon states that translations of children's books from English to French "outnumber those in the reverse direction by three to one." "Translation of Children's Books in Canada," *Canadian Children's Literature/ Littérature pour la jeunesse* 45 (1987): 14-53. The reader should also note that the proportion of articles in French is much greater than of reviews. The lack of reviews indicates the smaller number of works translated into French. For a contradictory analysis, see David Homel, "Le Traducteur dans la société," *Actes des deuxièmes assises de la traduction littéraire (Arles 1985)* (Arles, France: Actes Sud, 1986) 165-171.
9. Brault, 16.
10. See, for example, Philip Stratford, "Foreword/Préface," *Bibliography of Canadian Books in Translation/Bibliographie de livres canadiens traduits* (Ottawa: HRCC/CCRH, 1977) i-vii, ix-xvii; Richard Giguère, "Traduction littéraire et 'image' de la littérature au Canada et au Québec" *Translation in Canadian Literature: Symposium 1982*, Reappraisals: Canadian Writers 9, Camille R. La Bossière, ed. (Ottawa: University of Ottawa Press, 1983) 47-60; and "Translations: English to French," *The Oxford Companion to Canadian Literature* 794-795; and Jean Blouin, "Cette culture que nous ignorons," *L'Actualité* 5.3 (mars 1980): 32-39.
11. See David M. Hayne, "Literary Translation in Nineteenth-Century Canada," *Translation in Canadian Literature* 35-46.
12. Toronto: The Ryerson Press, 1960.
13. Montreal: nbj/Vancouver: Writing, 1986.
14. For more detailed histories of literary translation, see David Hayne, "Literary Translation in Nineteenth-Century Canada," *Translation in Canadian Literature* 35-46; Philip Stratford, "French-Canadian Literature in Translation," *Meta* 3.4 (décembre 1969): 180-187; "Foreword/Préface" to *Bibliography of Canadian Books in Translation/Bibliographie de livres canadiens traduits*; Richard Giguère, "Traduction littéraire et 'image' de la littérature au Canada et au Québec," *Translation in Canadian Literature* 47-60; Kathy Mezei, "A Bridge of Sorts: The Translation of Quebec Literature into English," *The Yearbook of English Studies* 15 (1985): 202-226; for more detailed discussions of translations from 1976 on, see the annual review of translations in *The University of Toronto Quarterly*, "Letters in Canada" number.
15. These have been retranslated by Alan Brown as *The Tin Flute*, John Glassco as *Fear's Folly*, and David Homel as *Broke City*.
16. "Quelques réflexions sur la traduction dans le contexte socio-culturel canado-québécois."
17. "How do you say 'Gabrielle Roy'?" *Translation in Canadian Literature* 13-34.

18. Stratford, "Literary Translation in Canada: A Survey," *Meta* 22.1 (mars 1977): 37-44; Claxton, "Translation and Creation," *Actes du colloque: traduction et qualité de langue* (Hull, Québec: Éditeur officiel du Québec, 1984) 74-78; Ellenwood, "Some Actualities of Canadian Literary Translation," *Translation in Canadian Literature* 61-72.

19. "Tradaptation" is a term used by Michel Garneau to resolve the dilemma of adaptation versus translation in theatrical productions. See Jean Delisle, "Dans les coulisses de l'adaptation théâtrale," *Circuit* 12 (mars 1986): 3-8; and Annie Brisset, "Institution théâtrale au Québec et problèmes théoriques de la traduction," *L'Institution littéraire* (Québec: IQRC/CRELIQ, 1986) 143-157.

20. See, for example, Evelyne Voldeng, "Trans Lata/Trans Latus," *TESSERA*, special number of *Room of One's Own* 8.4 (1984): 82-96; Susanne de Lotbinière-Harwood, "Les Belles Infidèles," *Arcade* 11 (février 1986): 22-25; Barbara Godard, "Language and Sexual Difference: The Case of Translation," *Atkinson Review of Canadian Studies* 2.1 (Fall/Winter 1984): 13-20.

21. See L.G. Kelly's Introduction, *The True Interpreter: A History of Translation, Theory and Practice in the West* (Oxford: Basil Blackwell, 1974) 1: "A complete theory of translation . . . has three components: specification of function and goal; description and analysis of operations, and critical comments on relationships between goal and operations."

22. See, however, for example, Susan Bassnet-McGuire, *Translation Studies*; Joseph E. Graham, ed., *Difference in Translation* (Ithaca: Cornell University Press, 1985); and Itamar Even-Zohar, "Polysystem Theory," *Poetics Today* 1.12 (Autumn 1979): 287-310; Gideon Toury, *In Search of a Theory of Translation* (Tel Aviv: Porter Institute for Poetics and Semiotics, 1980). Theo Herman describes a "new paradigm" in his "Introduction: Translation Studies and a New Paradigm": "Since about the mid-1970s, a loosely-knit international group of scholars has been attempting to break the deadlock in which the study of literary translation found itself . . . Their aim is . . . to establish a new paradigm for the study of literary translation, on the basis of a comprehensive theory and ongoing practical research . . . What they have in common is . . . a view of literature as a complex and dynamic system; a conviction that there should be a continual interplay between theoretical models and practical case studies; an approach to literary translation which is descriptive, target-oriented, functional and systematic; and an interest in the norms and constraints that govern the production and reception of translations, in the relation between translation and other types of text processing, and in the place and role of translation both within a given literature and in the interaction between literatures." *The Manipulation of Literature: Studies in Translation* (London: Croom Helm, 1985) 10-11.

23. "How do you say 'Gabrielle Roy'?" 17.

24. "Grounds for Translation," *Ellipse* 21 (1977): 58-91.

25. See *Poèmes des quatre côtés*.
26. See, for example, Itamar Even-Zohar, n. 22; and E.D. Blodgett, "Translation as a Key to Canadian Literature: Literary Translation and Literary System," *New Comparison* 1 (Summer 1986): 93-103.
27. Montreal: Guernica Editions, 1986, 17. Translation of Nicole Brossard's *Amantes*.

Introduction

OBJECTIFS

> As with medicine, literature and child psychology, everybody is an expert without even suspecting that there are things to be studied[1].

> Les mots nous choisissent autant que nous les choisissons, surtout ceux d'une langue étrangère[2].

Cette bibliographie embrasse la production critique sur la traduction littéraire au Canada dans les deux langues officielles, de 1950 à 1986. Même s'il s'est écrit beaucoup de choses au Canada sur la traduction au cours de cette période, nous n'en avons retenu que ce qui se rapportait à la traduction littéraire d'œuvres canadiennes en français et en anglais. Comme on peut s'en rendre compte d'après le nombre des entrées, cette partie des études sur la traduction littéraire[3] a peu à peu, mais constamment, évolué jusqu'à devenir un champ spécialisé de la critique, qui comprend des sujets aussi divers que la littérature comparée, la communication, la linguistique, la sociolinguistique, le féminisme, la politique et la création littéraire. C'est, par définition, une discipline mixte qui invite au flirt polysystématique et métatextuel (malgré la profession de fidélité de certains traducteurs). Par conséquent, l'art de la traduction littéraire, sa théorie et sa pratique ont attiré, comme on pouvait s'y attendre, un curieux mélange de praticiens, du dilettante à l'universitaire.

Cette bibliographie veut montrer non seulement la quantité de textes produits sur la traduction littéraire canadienne, mais aussi la qualité et la variété considérables de cette littérature. Certes, il reste encore beaucoup à faire et ce champ d'études en est tout juste à ses débuts dans ce pays. Quel peut être alors le principe directeur d'une telle bibliographie?

Il faut dire d'abord que notre entreprise vient à point, parce que la théorie et la critique de la traduction sont actuellement en train de s'établir sur des bases sérieuses. Il suffit pour s'en rendre compte de penser à l'avalanche des congrès, des tables rondes et des publications, aux activités de l'Association des traducteurs littéraires/Association of Literary Translators aussi bien au pays qu'ailleurs dans le monde et à la fondation de l'Association canadienne de traductologie.

Deuxièmement, cette bibliographie et ses annotations constituent, d'une part, un document historique qui répertorie l'ensemble et indique l'évolution de la littérature critique sur la traduction de la littérature canadienne en français et en anglais, tout en consignant l'histoire de la traduction littéraire moderne au Canada. D'autre part, ce travail appelle et prépare nécessairement le terrain à d'autres recherches qui combleront ses lacunes et, au besoin, ouvriront de nouvelles pistes.

Troisième point : comme il arrive souvent dans un champ d'études à la fois en plein essor et encore marginal, les documents se trouvent rarement situés là où l'on s'y attendrait. Puisse notre travail de « filature » faciliter la tâche des futurs chercheurs ou même des amateurs simplement curieux.

Enfin, la portée de cette bibliographie est liée aux retombées de l'effervescence littéraire des décennies 60 et 70 et se veut en même temps un hommage à l'audace et à l'inspiration des traducteurs qui ont su faire écho à cette renaissance, entraînant du même coup une progression spectaculaire de la traduction et de tout l'appareil critique qui l'accompagne sous forme de comptes rendus, d'articles et d'entrevues.

ÉTAT ET ÉVOLUTION DE LA RECHERCHE EN TRADUCTION LITTÉRAIRE
SUR DES ŒUVRES CANADIENNES EN FRANÇAIS ET EN ANGLAIS

Traduction

Dès 1534, la traduction orale faisait déjà partie intégrante de la vie politique et intellectuelle canadienne : c'est l'année où Jacques Cartier prit deux des fils du chef iroquois Donnacona pour les ramener avec lui en France où ils apprirent le français ; huit mois après, de retour au Nouveau Monde, ils agirent comme interprètes entre les Français et les Iroquois[4] à Stadaconé (c'est-à-dire à Québec). La traduction reçut un statut officiel par les dispositions linguistiques de l'Acte de l'Amérique du Nord britannique de 1867 et par la création en 1934 du Bureau fédéral des traductions. Le fonctionnement quotidien de la société canadienne est devenu indissociable de la traduction commerciale, technique et gouvernementale.

La nécessité de la traduction et ses implications au Québec en particulier ont engendré cependant de graves difficultés : la subordination d'une langue et d'une minorité culturelle à la langue et à la culture dominantes, l'érosion et la dégradation progressives de la langue ainsi dominée, avec toutes les conséquences que cela entraîne pour le caractère distinctif, la souveraineté culturelle et la volonté collective du groupe minoritaire[5].

Traduction littéraire

Contrairement à la traduction destinée au public en général, dont la nécessité a été légalement reconnue, la traduction littéraire s'est plutôt développée au gré des circonstances. Des écrivains se sont tournés vers la traduction littéraire, aiguillonnés par le défi lancé à leur créativité et pour le seul plaisir de s'attaquer à des difficultés de style et à des questions de langue : Philippe Aubert de Gaspé, Charles G.D. Roberts, F.R. Scott, John Glassco, Fred Cogswell, D.G. Jones, Daphne Marlatt, Claire Martin, Jacques Brault, Michel Beaulieu. Auteurs et traducteurs ont commencé à échanger des idées et à entrer en interaction : Anne Hébert et F.R. Scott, Gabrielle Roy et Joyce Marshall, Roch Carrier et Sheila Fischman, Jacques Ferron avec Ray Ellenwood et Betty Bednarski, Daphne Marlatt et Nicole Brossard.

Animés d'un zèle missionnaire, certains traducteurs ont tenté de convertir leur public aux charmes ou aux qualités de telle œuvre ou de tel écrivain dans l'autre langue. À la fin des années 50, 60 et au début des années 70, alors que la littérature québécoise était en pleine révolution tranquille et que l'indépendance semblait possible, l'activité des traducteurs, surtout du français vers l'anglais, atteignit rapidement son apogée.

Les traducteurs ont également été motivés par le rôle politique et culturel de la traduction littéraire. Comme le remarquait F.R. Scott dans la préface de ses *Poems of French Canada*, « translation is not only an art in itself, it is also an essential ingredient in Canada's political entity[6] ». De plus en plus, traducteurs, auteurs et commentateurs décrivent la traduction littéraire comme un pont jeté entre les deux solitudes et les traducteurs se voient comme des médiateurs culturels. Pourtant, la demande et le volume de traduction sont la preuve paradoxale du fait brutal de ces deux solitudes. De plus, la densité de la circulation sur ce pont imaginaire est bien moindre dans le sens qui va du Canada anglais vers le Québec que dans le sens contraire. Dans son article du *Oxford Companion to Canadian Literature*, « Translations: French to English[7] », John O'Connor prétend que, jusqu'à 1983, 550 œuvres littéraires ont été traduites du français vers l'anglais, mais seulement 400 l'ont été de l'anglais vers le français. La présente bibliographie montre la même chose : moins de 20% des entrées en langue française prouvent que le Québec s'intéresse peu aux traductions faites à partir de l'anglais[8]. Comme l'écrit Jacques Brault en commentaire dans ses *Poèmes des quatre côtés*, « nous n'aimons ni traduire ni être traduits : les clefs de la traduction appartiennent aux puissants[9] ». Plusieurs critiques, en français et en anglais, ont signalé ces décevantes statistiques et tenté quelques explications[10]. Si l'isolement volontaire du Québec, son appréhension de l'impérialisme anglais et sa préférence pour la littérature américaine, plutôt que canadienne, peuvent compter parmi quelques-unes des explications, la question mérite dans son ensemble une enquête plus approfondie.

Bien que la traduction littéraire n'ait pas été un aspect négligeable de la vie littéraire du XIXe siècle et du début du XX[e11], et que plusieurs écrivains majeurs—qu'on pense aux Québécois Gabrielle Roy, Roger Lemelin, Ringuet, Félix-Antoine Savard—aient tous été traduits au cours des années 40, c'est surtout après la Seconde Guerre mondiale qu'on peut noter une augmentation graduelle du nombre des traductions, de même qu'une augmentation du nombre des revues littéraires qui allaient ouvrir des débouchés tant aux traducteurs qu'aux critiques.

En 1960, P.F. Widdows publia sa traduction de *Poèmes choisis d'Émile Nelligan*[12] après que Jean Beaupré et Gael Turnbull eurent lancé leurs traductions de Saint-Denys Garneau, Roland Giguère, Gilles Hénault et Paul-Marie Lapointe dans la collection de Contact Press, au cours des années 50. Les traductions de Saint-Denys Garneau par F.R. Scott parurent d'abord dans *The Tamarack Review* 4 (1957), celles des poètes québécois Pierre Trottier, Anne Hébert, Jean-Guy Pilon, Roland Giguère et Gilles Hénault dans *The Tamarack Review* 7 (1958); et *St. Denys Garneau and Anne Hébert* fut publié par Klanak Press en 1962.

La révolution thématique et formelle du « nouveau roman », qui fit irruption sur la scène littéraire québécoise pendant les années 60, suscita l'intérêt du Canada anglais et stimula la traduction; les romans d'Hubert Aquin, Gérard Bessette, Marie-Claire Blais, Jacques Godbout, Claude Jasmin, André Langevin, Jacques Renaud furent traduits, bien qu'assez lentement, avec trois ou quatre ans de décalage entre l'original et la version anglaise. Par contre, seuls Stephen Leacock, Hugh MacLennan et Margaret Laurence (et Mazo de la Roche) parurent en version française à la même époque. Parmi les dramaturges des deux langues, seul Gratien Gélinas avait été traduit en 1969.

En 1972, la traduction avait augmenté le volume de ses activités et elle avait reçu aussi une reconnaissance officielle ainsi qu'un appui par la mise sur pied du Programme de subvention des traductions du Conseil des arts du Canada. C'est en 1973 que les prix de traduction du Conseil des arts furent créés; l'Association des traducteurs littéraires/Association of Literary Translators était fondée deux ans plus tard. De petites maisons d'édition canadiennes-anglaises, telles Anansi, Oberon, Talonbooks, Coach House Press, de concert avec les éditeurs les mieux établis, McClelland and Stewart et General Publishing, étaient prêtes à publier des livres en traduction et même, dans le cas des petites maisons d'édition, des traductions de textes d'avant-garde. Harvest House, une maison anglophone de Montréal, qui a publié *Ethel and the Terrorist* de Claude Jasmin (traduction de David S. Walker, 1965), a commencé à publier régulièrement sa collection « French Writers of Canada » dans les années 70. La première livraison d'*Ellipse*, revue consacrée à la publication d'ouvrages en traduction, parut en 1969, et l'anthologie fracassante de John Glassco, *Poetry of French Canada in Translation*, fut publiée en 1970, aussitôt suivie des recueils de Fred Cogswell, *One Hundred Poems of Modern Quebec* (1970) et *A Second Hundred Poems of Modern Quebec* (1971).

Au Québec, Le Cercle du Livre de France lança sa « Collection des Deux solitudes » en 1973, faisant ainsi connaître Morley Callaghan, Robertson Davies, Margaret Laurence, Mordecai Richler, Brian Moore, W.O. Mitchell. Plusieurs écrivains—Leonard Cohen, Mordecai Richler, Audrey Thomas, Malcolm Lowry—avaient été publiés en France.

La première édition de *Bibliography of Canadian Books in Translation/Bibliographie de livres canadiens traduits* indispensable de Philip Stratford et Maureen Newman a paru en 1975, témoignant ainsi de l'importance croissante de la traduction littéraire.

Certains changements importants se sont produits dans les années 80. Plus d'éditeurs québécois sont entrés sur le marché de la traduction : Québec/Amérique, Éditions HMH, Fides, Héritage, L'Étincelle, Les Éditions Leméac ; la poésie contemporaine est davantage traduite en anglais grâce à l'initiative d'éditeurs comme Guernica Editions, Véhicule Press, Coach House Press, Exile Editions ; la traduction et la création de pièces de théâtre ont augmenté pendant que le décalage diminue entre la parution de l'original et celle du texte traduit. La production québécoise féministe commence à retenir l'attention par les récentes traductions de Nicole Brossard, Louky Bersianik et Jovette Marchessault. Certaines expériences de traduction, comme *Ellipse 8x8* (29/30, 1982), où quatre poètes anglophones et quatre poètes francophones ont traduit réciproquement chacun quatre poèmes à la suite, ou comme les intertextes ou « transformations » de Daphne Marlatt et Nicole Brossard, *Mauve* et *Jeu de lettres/Characters*[13], ces recherches marquent une nouvelle étape. Les traducteurs de textes difficiles, Ray Ellenwood (l'automatiste Claude Gauvreau), Barbara Godard (Nicole Brossard), Patricia Claxton (Nicole Brossard) signent eux-mêmes la préface de leurs traductions en y décrivant leur façon de procéder[14].

Critique de la traduction
L'examen diachronique du matériel critique recoupe l'histoire des attitudes à l'endroit du bilinguisme, de l'autre solitude, de l'art et de la pratique de la traduction littéraire.

Bien que certaines revues aient été réceptives à la traduction et aux comptes rendus de livres traduits à la fin des années 50 et pendant les années 60, par exemple *The Tamarack Review, Prism International, Liberté*, la traduction n'en était pas moins considérée avec suspicion et on consacrait beaucoup de pages à la justifier. Les signataires de comptes rendus étaient souvent unilingues, commentaient le texte sans mentionner le nom du traducteur ni même le fait qu'il s'agissait d'une traduction. J'ai même trouvé un ou deux comptes rendus dont l'auteur affirmait que les traductions étaient médiocres alors qu'il n'avait pas lu et ne pouvait même pas lire l'original !

Nos annotations font ressortir la récurrence de certaines remarques du reste prévisibles, dont les suivantes :
1. la difficulté de traduire la poésie
2. la difficulté de traduire (surtout du français vers l'anglais) la langue dialectale, les jurons, le niveau vernaculaire et le *joual*
3. le problème épineux des titres
4. la fidélité au ton ou à l'esprit du texte original
5. la démarcation incertaine entre traduction libre, fidèle ou littérale
6. la présence d'un contresens patent

Toutefois, à la fin des années 60 et au cours des années 70, suite à l'institutionnalisation de la traduction par le Conseil des arts et par les collections spécialisées des éditeurs, l'appareil critique entourant la traduction s'est développé. D'abord les traducteurs et les auteurs de comptes rendus ont cessé de se sentir obligés de se justifier et ont commencé à s'interroger sur leurs façons de procéder. De nombreux critiques bilingues en mesure de comparer rigoureusement l'original et la version sont apparus ; plusieurs d'entre eux étaient également traducteurs : Gwladys Downes, Philip Stratford, D.G. Jones furent de ceux qui fournirent des exposés pénétrants sur les textes traduits, évitant de résumer l'intrigue pour donner plutôt au lecteur une appréciation fouillée à l'intérieur d'un cadre théorique.

Le plaidoyer a toujours été le leitmotiv des commentaires critiques : montrer la nécessité d'une aide institutionnelle, encourager la demande de traductions, établir l'importance de la traduction comme pont entre deux cultures et déplorer le manque de traductions des textes classiques ou d'importance capitale. Critiques et traducteurs ont également insisté sans cesse sur le besoin de traducteurs compétents et de nouvelles traductions d'œuvres déjà traduites : *The Tin Flute* de Gabrielle Roy (par Hannah Josephson), *Sackcloth for Banner* de Jean-Charles Harvey (par Lukin Barette) et *Flat, Broke and Beat* de Jacques Renaud (par Gérald Robitaille)[15]. Il semble que chaque génération doive évidemment retraduire en fonction de ses propres attentes.

Le remarquable virage des années 80 vers la métatraduction, par où le discours sur la méthodologie s'insère dans le texte publié ou l'accompagne, comme, par exemple, dans les éditions bilingues de la maison

Guernica, les commentaires de la livraison d'*Ellipse 8x8*, le nombre croissant de préfaces explicatives signées par le traducteur, tout cela reflète des changements quant au statut et à l'objet des recherches en traduction. Différentes stratégies ont été récemment entreprises. Devant les œuvres postmodernes et féministes, les auteurs de comptes rendus et les critiques ont été obligés de réviser des notions comme la traduction littérale (littéralité sémantique ou syntaxique ?), l'inscription du genre et de la différence sexuelle tant dans la langue de départ que dans la langue d'arrivée et dans les mécanismes de transmission de l'une à l'autre. Soulevant la question du contexte en traduction, Ben-Zion Shek[16] et E.D. Blodgett[17] ont signalé les dangers inhérents de la traduction dans un pays où la diglossie est répandue. Philip Stratford, Patricia Claxton et Ray Ellenwood[18] ont étudié l'histoire souvent lacunaire de la traduction littéraire et analysé la politique du gouvernement fédéral.

Cette perspective nous permet par conséquent de voir que les études en traduction se ramifient apparemment selon les subdivisions suivantes : histoire, culture et politique, critique littéraire et littérature comparée, théorie, pratique, adaptation et « tradaptation[19] », et genre[20].

C'est l'augmentation de ce que E.D. Blodgett appellerait « Canadian meditations », augmentation vérifiable par la publication de modestes articles sur la traduction littéraire dans les revues, par la revue annuelle de la traduction dans *The University of Toronto Quarterly*, par les colloques et les actes des débats universitaires, comme *Translation in Canadian Literature* (1983) et *La Traduction : l'universitaire et le praticien* (1984), qui marque le véritable démarrage des études canadiennes en traduction. Le nombre des ouvrages qui étaient en cours de préparation lors de la mise sous presse de cette bibliographie témoigne également de l'essor de cette discipline : un prochain numéro spécial de *Canadian Literature* (117, printemps 1988) et de *Translation Review* (Dallas) ; la monumentale histoire de la traduction de Jean Delisle, *La Traduction au Canada/Translation in Canada 1534-1984* (Ottawa: Les Presses de l'Université d'Ottawa, 1987) ; l'édition prochaine des actes du congrès d'octobre 1986 de l'Association des traducteurs littéraires, « Literary Translation and Literary Identity », chez Véhicule Press ; les actes de la table ronde sur les rapports entre auteur et traducteur, lors du colloque « Les Femmes et les mots », en 1983, à paraître dans *Meta* ; une séance spéciale sur la traduction au colloque Malcolm Lowry en mai 1987 ; certaines séances aussi de l'Association canadienne de littérature comparée aux Congrès des sociétés savantes de 1986 et 1987. Depuis 1981, deux nouveaux prix de traduction ont été inaugurés : le Prix de traduction John Glassco et le Prix de traduction F.R. Scott, en l'honneur de deux pionniers de la traduction littéraire.

CE QUI RESTE À FAIRE

En même temps qu'elle coïncide avec l'indéniable affirmation de ce champ d'études, cette bibliographie en dévoile aussi les lacunes. Quels développements à venir apparaissent souhaitables au point où nous en sommes aujourd'hui ?

1. *Théorie et terminologie :* bien que la théorie de la traduction[21] se fonde sur la linguistique comparée et qu'elle soit relativement bien formulée, la traduction littéraire par contre est loin d'être aussi avancée[22]. Dans le même ordre d'idée, comme le signale E.D. Blodgett, « Canadian meditations on translation are neither as plentiful nor as various as they might be[23] ». Six thèses de maîtrise sur trente-sept, qui sont des traductions, ne comportent aucun commentaire sur la théorie de la traduction ni sur la pratique du traducteur dans leur introduction, ce qui est assez intéressant. Jusqu'à maintenant, les approches théoriques se sont intéressées à :

(i) l'examen des vertus respectives de la traduction libre, littérale ou fidèle

(ii) le concept de « effective communion[24] » selon D.G. Jones— version sophistiquée de l'idée de pont entre deux cultures

(iii) la description par Jacques Brault de sa pratique comme une « nontraduction[25] »—application créatrice du principe du laisser-faire à la traduction poétique

(iv) la traduction comprise comme un polysystème et la traduction dans le polysystème de la littérature, ce qui constitue une adaptation au contexte canadien, par E.D. Blodgett, du concept de littérature mis au point par Itamar Even-Zohar qui soutient que la littérature consiste en un « conglomerate of systems » complexe et dynamique[26].

Il faut que la critique en arrive à construire, comme Annie Brisset, E.D. Blodgett, Sherry Simon s'y emploient couramment, des modèles théoriques opératoires pour analyser la complexité des réseaux d'interactions qu'implique la traduction littéraire au Canada. « Traduction fidèle », « justesse du ton », « ne rend pas justice à l'original » sont autant de lieux communs éculés qui trahissent la médiocrité de l'analyse et qui ne disent rien des prouesses d'imagination ni des opérations complexes auxquelles se livrent les traducteurs. Il nous faut aller plus avant. Au lieu de relever platement les contresens, la critique devrait s'appliquer à scruter la nature et le sens des erreurs et des écarts.

2. *Études à faire du rôle politique et culturel de la traduction littéraire :* les questions à résoudre sont : (i) qui traduit-on ? (et qui ne traduit-on pas ?) ; (ii) le rôle des institutions comme le Conseil des arts, les éditeurs et les directeurs littéraires, l'Association des traducteurs litté-

raires, la revue *Ellipse* (qui traduit-on et qui traduit ? quelles sont les politiques éditoriales et les politiques de traduction ?).

3. *Les pratiques de traduction :* l'étude des pratiques de traduction, tant dans le décodage du texte de départ que dans l'encodage du texte d'arrivée, l'analyse des décisions qui touchent, par exemple, le choix des expressions anglaises en rapport avec le texte de départ en français, ou les équivalences des régionalismes, jurons, locutions en joual. L'importance des notes du traducteur ou des préfaces est capitale pour la documentation des procédés de traduction. Comme le signale Barbara Godard dans sa « Preface » à *Lovhers :* « One could write a history of theories of translation, a history of the relationships between author and translator, indeed between author and reader by writing a history of the preface as genre[27] ». Il nous faut, en d'autres mots, des études en profondeur sur les fonctions de la lecture et de l'écriture dans le processus de traduction.

4. *Des perspectives historiques sur la traduction littéraire :* des études sur la traduction littéraire à différentes époques et sur l'histoire de la traduction d'un texte en particulier ou sur les différentes versions d'un même texte traduit ; par exemple, *Maria Chapdelaine.*

5. *Études à entreprendre :* sur « l'opérationalité » de la théorie du polysystème ; sur l'inscription des différences sexuelles ; sur l'adaptation théâtrale ; sur la traduction en rapport avec l'intertextualité et la métatextualité ; sur les rapports entre auteur et traducteur et sur la traduction en tant que lecture et en tant qu'interprétation.

NOTES À L'INTENTION DE L'USAGER

Périodisation et mise en forme typographique de la bibliographie
Cette bibliographie couvre les années 1950 à 1986. La date de 1950 s'imposait comme point de départ à cause de l'importance accrue de la traduction littéraire après la Seconde Guerre mondiale. Le protocole de présentation matérielle est celui du *MLA Style Manual* (1985), que nous avons suivi pour les entrées tant en langue française qu'en langue anglaise, pour des raisons de cohérence, à une exception près : les comptes rendus de traductions comportent leurs références complètes—lieu de publication, éditeur et année de publication—de façon à fournir à l'usager toute l'information disponible pour ses propres besoins.

Annotations
Il s'agit d'un commentaire descriptif, non d'une paraphrase, excluant tout jugement de valeur.

Catégories
Les rubriques sous lesquelles la critique sur la traduction littéraire a été répartie sont les suivantes : *articles, bibliographies, livres, entrevues, introductions* (y compris toute préface, avertissement, postface, notes de présentation du traducteur, introduction de l'éditeur), *comptes rendus de fond, comptes rendus* (uniquement ceux qui **évaluent** les traductions d'une façon détaillée et qui comportent généralement des exemples) ; *thèses, notes des traducteurs* (notes élaborées et **incorporées** au texte traduit).

Nous n'avons pas, sauf en appendice, inclus ce qui touche à la littérature pour enfants.

Méthodologie
La traduction littéraire au Canada est ce qui a servi de critère au choix des entrées ; toutes les références répertoriées ont été examinées.

Toute bibliographie joue sur une série d'opérateurs qui va de l'enquête systématique à l'intuition, en passant par le concours de circonstances. Un coup d'œil furtif sur un rayon de bibliothèque peut parfois conduire à dénicher un article pertinent. Les microfiches et les bases de données, même si elles sont utiles et qu'elles économisent un temps précieux, ne peuvent jamais dispenser de feuilleter les revues, de fouiller les greniers, ni de solliciter les précieux conseils des collègues.

Nos sources proviennent des répertoires bibliographiques ordinaires, mais ne s'y limitent pas : *Canadian Periodical Index ; Canadian Essay and Literature Index ; Radar ; Périodex ; Point de repère ; Index Translationum ; Canadian Book Review Annual ; Canadian Literature Index ;* et les bibliographies : *MLA Bibliography ; Bibliography of Canadian Books in Translation/Bibliographie de livres canadiens traduits* (1977) ; la collection de Hayne-Sirois, « Preliminary Bibliography of Comparative Canadian Literature » ; *International Bibliography of Translation: Index;* « Annual Bibliography of Commonwealth Literature » ; la collection « Canadian Literature/Littérature canadienne : an annotated bibliography/une bibliographie avec commentaire », préparée par Bruce Nesbitt ; la bibliographie de *La Revue d'histoire littéraire du Québec et du Canada français.*

Index
Au début de chaque index, l'usager trouvera les explications ou instructions utiles. On notera aussi que la terminologie de la traduction n'apparaît que rarement dans l'index, bien qu'elle existe en théorie et qu'elle soit même fort développée. La raison en est bien simple : c'est que la critique ne l'utilise pas et qu'elle est par conséquent inexistante dans le matériel répertorié. L'index des sujets en français contient un plus grand nombre de termes techniques, plusieurs étant empruntés à Jean-Paul Vinay et Jean

Darbelnet dans *Stylistique comparée du français et de l'anglais* (Paris: Didier, 1958). Je voudrais enfin attirer l'attention du lecteur sur la fameuse formule de Wittgenstein : « the meaning of a word is its use in the language », en soulignant le fait évident que la traduction est d'abord affaire de langue et qu'une bonne partie de la critique vise naturellement l'aspect linguistique ; beaucoup d'entrées de l'index des sujets sont donc apparentées à la langue, bien que le mot « langue » ne soit pas lui-même une entrée. Les entrées explicitement liées à la langue sont : compétence linguistique ; contexte linguistique ; dialecte ; expressions anglaises, ce qu'il en advient dans la traduction anglaise du français ; expressions anglaises, présence dans le texte français ; erreurs lexicales ; faux amis ; français, formes différentes du ; français, sa reproduction en traduction anglaise ; intraduisibilité linguistique ; néologismes.

Renvois
Afin d'éviter la lourdeur d'un système de renvois, nous orientons plutôt l'usager vers les index. Seuls les articles qui comportent des références à d'autres articles ou à des comptes rendus et les ouvrages écrits en collaboration font l'objet de renvois.

Traduit par Réjean Beaudoin

NOTES

1. Itamar Even-Zohar, "Translation Theory Today," *Poetics Today* 2.4 (1981): 1.
2. Jacques Brault, *Poèmes des quatre côtés* (Saint-Lambert: Éditions du Noroît, 1975) 14.
3. Susan Bassnet-McGuire, citant une formule d'André Lefevere, définit les études sur la traduction comme "the discipline that concerns itself with problems raised by the production and description of translations." *Translation Studies* (London: Methuen, 1983) 1.
4. Jean Delisle, "Les Pionniers de l'interprétation au Canada," *Meta* 22.1 (mars 1977): 5-15.
5. *Cf.* Pierre Chantefort, *Diglossie au Québec; limites et tendances actuelles* (Québec: Les Presses de l'Université Laval, 1970); Ben-Zion Shek, "Quelques réflexions sur la traduction dans le contexte socio-culturel canado-québécois," *Ellipse* 21 (1977): 111-117.
6. Burnaby: Blackfish Press, 1977, vi.
7. Toronto: Oxford, 1983, 795-796.
8. André Gagnon déclare cependant que la traduction des livres pour enfants de l'anglais vers le français "outnumber[s] those in the reverse direction by three

to one." "Translation of Children's Books in Canada," *Canadian Children's Literature/Littérature pour la jeunesse* 45 (1987): 14-53. Le lecteur notera que la proportion des articles en langue française est beaucoup plus grande que celle des comptes rendus. Le manque de comptes rendus est un indice du plus petit nombre d'œuvres traduites en français. Pour une analyse contradictoire, voir David Homel, "Le Traducteur dans la societé," *Actes des deuxièmes assises de la traduction littéraire (Arles 1985)* (Arles, France: Actes Sud, 1986) 165-171.

9. Brault, 16.

10. *Cf.*, par exemple, Philip Stratford, "Foreword/Préface," *Bibliography of Canadian Books in Translation/Bibliographie de livres canadiens traduits* (Ottawa: CCRH/HRCC, 1977): i-vii, ix-xvii; Richard Giguère, "Traduction littéraire et 'image' de la littérature au Canada et au Québec," *Translation in Canadian Literature: Symposium 1982*, Reappraisals: Canadian Writers 9, Camille R. La Bossière, ed. (Ottawa: University of Ottawa Press, 1983) 47-60; et "Translations: English to French," *The Oxford Companion to Canadian Literature* 794-795; aussi Jean Blouin, "Cette culture que nous ignorons," *L'Actualité* 5.3 (mars 1980): 32-39.

11. *Cf.* David M. Hayne, "Literary Translation in Nineteenth-Century Canada," *Translation in Canadian Literature* 35-46.

12. Toronto: The Ryerson Press, 1960.

13. Montréal: nbj/Vancouver: Writing, 1986.

14. Pour une histoire plus détaillée de la traduction littéraire, *cf.* David Hayne, "Literary Translation in Nineteenth-Century Canada," *Translation in Canadian Literature* 35-46; Philip Stratford, "French-Canadian Literature in Translation," *Meta* 3.4 (décembre 1969): 180-187; "Foreword/Préface," *Bibliography of Canadian Books in Translation/Bibliographie de livres canadiens traduits*; Richard Giguère, "Traduction littéraire et 'image' de la littérature au Canada et au Québec," *Translation in Canadian Literature* 47-60; Kathy Mezei, "A Bridge of Sorts: The Translation of Quebec Literature into English," *The Yearbook of English Studies* 15 (1985): 202-226; pour l'étude approfondie de la traduction depuis 1976, consulter la revue annuelle des traductions dans *The University of Toronto Quarterly*, numéro "Letters in Canada."

15. Tous ces livres ont effectivement été retraduits: *The Tin Flute* par Alan Brown, *Fear's Folly* par John Glassco et *Broke City* par David Homel.

16. "Quelques réflexions sur la traduction dans le contexte socio-culturel canado-québécois."

17. "How do you say 'Gabrielle Roy'?" *Translation in Canadian Literature* 13-34.

18. Stratford, "Literary Translation in Canada: A Survey," *Meta* 22.1 (mars 1977): 37-44; Claxton, "Translation and Creation," *Actes du colloque: traduction et qualité de langue* (Hull, Québec: Éditeur officiel du Québec, 1984) 74-78;

Ellenwood, "Some Actualities of Canadian Literary Translation," *Translation in Canadian Literature* 61-72.

19. Le mot "tradaptation" est un néologisme créé par Michel Garneau pour tâcher de résoudre le dilemme "adaptation vs traduction" dans la production dramatique. *Cf.* Jean Delisle, "Dans les coulisses de l'adaptation théâtrale," *Circuit* 12 (mars 1986): 3-8; et Annie Brisset, "Institution théâtrale au Québec et problèmes théoriques de la traduction," *L'Institution littéraire* (Québec: IQRC/ CRELIQ, 1986) 143-157.

20. *Cf.*, par exemple, Evelyne Voldeng, "Trans Lata/Trans Latus," *TESSERA*, special number of *Room of One's Own* 8.4 (1984): 83-96; Susanne de Lotbinière-Harwood, "Les Belles Infidèles," *Arcade* 11 (février 1986): 22-25; Barbara Godard, "Language and Sexual Difference: The Case of Translation," *Atkinson Review of Canadian Studies* 2.1 (Fall/Winter 1984): 13-20.

21. *Cf.* l'introduction de L.G. Kelly à *The True Interpreter: A History of Translation, Theory and Practice in the West* (Oxford: Basil Blackwell, 1974) 1: "A complete theory of translation . . . has three components: specification of function and goal; description and analysis of operations, and critical comments on relationships between goal and operations."

22. Consulter cependant, par exemple, Susan Bassnet-McGuire, *Translation Studies*; Joseph E. Graham, ed., *Difference in Translation* (Ithaca: Cornell University Press, 1985); et Itamar Even-Zohar, "Polysystem Theory," *Poetics Today* 1.12 (Autumn 1979): 287-310; Gideon Toury, *In Search of a Theory of Translation* (Tel Aviv: Porter Institute for Poetics and Semiotics, 1980). Theo Herman décrit un nouveau paradigme dans son "Introduction: Translation Studies and a New Paradigm": "Since about the mid-1970s, a loosely-knit international group of scholars has been attempting to break the deadlock in which the study of literary translation found itself . . . Their aim is . . . to establish a new paradigm for the study of literary translation, on the basis of a comprehensive theory and ongoing practical research . . . What they have in common is . . . a view of literature as a complex and dynamic system; a conviction that there should be a continual interplay between theoretical models and practical case studies; an approach to literary translation which is descriptive, target-oriented, functional and systematic; and an interest in the norms and constraints that govern the production and reception of translations, in the relation between translation and other types of text processing, and in the place and role of translation both within a given literature and in the interaction between literatures." *The Manipulation of Literature: Studies in Translation* (London: Croom Helm, 1985) 10-11.

23. "How do you say 'Gabrielle Roy'?" 17.

24. "Grounds for Translation," *Ellipse* 21 (1977): 58-91.

25. *Poèmes des quatre côtés.*

26. *Cf.*, par exemple, Itamar Even-Zohar, n. 22; et E.D. Blodgett, "Translation as a Key to Canadian Literature: Literary Translation and Literary System," *New Comparison* 1 (Summer 1986): 93-103.
27. Montréal: Guernica Editions, 1986, 17. Traduction des *Amantes* de Nicole Brossard.

1. Amprimoz, Alexandre. "Traduire la poésie soi-disant hermétique: l'exemple de l'œuvre de Cécile Cloutier." *La Traduction: l'universitaire et le praticien.* Cahiers de traductologie, No 5. Édit. Arlette Thomas et Jacques Flamand. Congrès: Université du Québec à Montréal, 28-31 mai 1980. Ottawa: Éditions de l'Université d'Ottawa, 1984. 197-202.

   Décrit à l'aide d'exemples précis le difficile et délicat processus de la traduction de *Springtime of Spoken Words* (1979); contient la réponse de Cloutier; réfléchit sur le fait de traduire de la poésie et la nature de cette traduction; compare la création poétique et la traduction.

2. Baudot, Alain. "L'Actualité," "Tables rondes: I-Écrivains et traducteurs/Writers vs Translators." *Meta* 26.2 (juin 1981): 204-205.

   Compte rendu d'une table ronde, colloque de Glendon, 1980, avec Martine De Clercq, Derrick De Kerckhove, Ray Ellenwood, Barbara Godard, Cliff Hanley, Hanne Martinet, Jean-Claude Masson, Yves Velan (Animateur: Naïm Kattan).

   La table ronde s'intéresse surtout à la traduction littéraire qu'elle analyse et illustre avec des exemples; résume la discussion centrée sur les relations existant entre les textes de départ et d'arrivée, l'auteur et le traducteur, la traduction en tant que création et écriture.

3. Baudry, René. "Histoire et traductions." *Revue d'histoire de l'Amérique française* 10.3 (décembre 1956): 305-309.

   Examine plusieurs cas de traduction de documents historiques, s'intéressant surtout à l'exemple frappant du *Pioneers of France in the New World* de Francis Parkman, dans lequel plusieurs historiens ont mal lu le nom d'un bateau (1613) et ont traduit *Mayflower* par *La Fleur de May*.

4. Beaulieu, Nicole. "La Voix discrète d'une traductrice de fond." *L'Actualité* 11.12 (décembre 1986): 157-159.

   Retrace la carrière de la traductrice Sheila Fischman.

5. Bednarski, Betty. "Teaching French-Canadian Literature in Translation." *Journal of Education* 6.4 (1980): 13-16.

   Explains the importance of translation in teaching French-Canadian literature to anglophones; discusses the current state of literary translation; reflects on how widely translations are sold and read.

6. Belcher, Margaret. "Les Fous de Bassan/In the Shadow of the Wind." *Canadian Literature* 109 (Summer 1986): 159-165.

Detailed description of the significance of the title of Hébert's novel in the source text and in Fischman's translation, the difference between the two, and how the English title is, in comparison, only "an aborted metaphor."

7. Binsse, Harry Lorin. "An Intellectual Iron Curtain?" *The Montreal Star* (11 May 1962): 2.

Written in response to Walter O'Hearn's article, "Too Deep for Tears or Mirth" [see 101], which asked pertinent questions regarding the "intellectual iron curtain" that separates English- and French-speaking Canadians; claims that the problem is "primarily . . . economic"; outlines the costs involved in relation to both the translator and publisher; discusses the problem of Canada's particular language situation and the necessity that a translator be familiar "with these often admirably expressive localisms"; claims that "language barriers are even more complex for the French side"; includes a list of the translations available in both languages, emphasizes the cultural role of translation and suggests that the Canada Council develop a "wholly systematic and inclusive" programme for increased translation.

8. Blodgett, E.D. "How do you say 'Gabrielle Roy'?" *Translation in Canadian Literature: Symposium 1982*. Reappraisals: Canadian Writers 9. Ed. Camille R. La Bossière. Ottawa: University of Ottawa Press, 1983. 13-34.

Addresses, within a wide historical and cultural context, theoretical issues facing translators of the two "founding" literatures, referring particularly to theories of D.G. Jones [see 70] and Jacques Brault [see 174]; argues that otherness and difference between two cultures should be preserved through translation.

9. Blodgett, Edward [E.D.]. "Translation as a Key to Canadian Literature: Literary Translation and Literary System." *New Comparison: A Journal of Comparative and General Literary Studies* 1 (Summer 1986): 93-103.

Outlines the history and current state of literary translation in Canada; examines the role of translators and translation in literary exchange between Quebec and English-Canadian "polysystems," with examples from D.G. Jones, "Grounds for Translation" [see 70], and Jacques Brault, *Poèmes des quatre côtés* [see 174].

10. Blouin, Jean. "Cette culture que nous ignorons." *L'Actualité* 5.3 (mars 1980): 32-39.

   Commentaire sur la traduction faisant partie de "l'échange inégal" entre le Canada anglais et le Québec.

11. Bonenfant, Jean-Charles. "L'Influence de la littérature canadienne-anglaise au Canada français." *The Making of Modern Poetry in Canada: Essential Articles on Contemporary Canadian Poetry in English*. Ed. Louis Dudek et Michael Gnarowski. Toronto: The Ryerson Press, 1967. 256-264. Réimpression tirée de *Culture* 17.3 (septembre 1956): 251-260.

   Commente le rôle que joue la traduction dans la connaissance qu'ont les deux cultures de la littérature et de la culture de l'autre.

12. Bonenfant, Joseph. Voir 86.

13. Brault, Jacques. "Remarques sur la traduction de la poésie/Some Notes on the Translation of Poetry." Trans. Sheila Fischman. *Ellipse* 21 (1977): 10-35.

   Expose ses théories sur la traduction de la poésie; parle de son concept de nontraduction; constate que "traduire un poème, c'est proprement écrire un poème relatif à une expérience de lecture poétique, donc de lecture qui n'est pas elle-même traductrice (au sens péjoratif)"; suggère que "le temps est arrivé, pour les poètes québécois, de pratiquer sans vergogne les démarches d'appropriation, de vol à l'étalage, de trahison et de détournement de sens qu'implique la traduction de la poésie." Signale les contradictions dans la critique "très indulgente" qu'a faite Noël Audet de ses *Poèmes des quatre côtés* [voir 174; 277].

   Outlines his theories on the translation of poetry, refers to his concept of "nontraduction"; states that "translating a poem . . . is writing a poem that relates to an experience of poetic reading"; suggests that "the poets of Quebec" should "move boldly towards the appropriation, shoplifting, treason and the twisting of meaning implied in the translation of poetry." Points out contradictions in Noël Audet's "very indulgent" review of his *Poèmes des quatre côtés* [see 174; 277].

14. Brierley, Jane. "Philippe-Joseph Aubert de Gaspé: One of our Earliest and Most Famous Official Translators." *Circuit* 13 (septembre 1986): 15-16.

Describes Aubert de Gaspé's *Mémoires* of which she is doing an annotated translation, his knowledge of English, and his job as an official translator in the province of Lower Canada in 1813-1816.

15. Brierre, Jacques. "Maria Chapdelaine: études linguistique et comparée (traductions anglaises)." Texte inédit. Université de Montréal, Département d'études françaises, 1968. Le fonds d'archives de Nicole Deschamps (p. 169). Service des archives de l'Université de Montréal.

Traite en détail de la traduction faite par W.H. Blake du *Maria Chapdelaine* de Louis Hémon, s'attachant à certains "mots-clés"; donne des exemples de contresens; suggère que Blake a manqué des nuances importantes, donc trahi l'original. Au contraire de Paré [voir 105], ne compare pas les traductions de Blake et d'Andrew Macphail.

16. Brisset, Annie. "Traduit au Québec: 'Ceci n'est pas une trahison.'" *Spirale* 62 (été 1986): 12-13.

Décrit l'évolution de la traduction du théâtre au Québec vers l'adaptation, l'importance culturelle de la traduction au Québec qui permet "d'être dit par l'Autre" et comment le *Macbeth* de Michel Garneau est "traduit en québécois."

17. Brisset, Annie. "Institution théâtrale au Québec et problèmes théoriques de la traduction." *L'Institution littéraire*. Sous la direction de Maurice Lemire avec l'assistance de Michel Cord. Actes du colloque organisé par l'Institut québécois de recherche sur la culture et le Centre de recherche en littérature québécoise, 1986. Québec: IQRC/CRELIQ, 1986. 143-157.

Essaie de dégager les codes institutionnels qui recouvrent les stratégies de traduction dans un espace socio-culturel donné, employant la traduction de *Macbeth* par Michel Garneau et de *Oncle Vania* par Michel Tremblay.

18. Brisset, Annie. "Vive la traduction . . . libre!" *Circuit* 12 (mars 1986): 10.

Déclare qu'au Québec, le théâtre est le genre privilégié de la traduction littéraire depuis 20 ans, et qu'il y a émergence de la nouvelle dramaturgie québécoise employant la langue vernaculaire et traduisant des pièces américaines, Tchekhov, Gogol, Brecht, *Macbeth*.

19. Brodeur, Léo-A. "Why I am a Translator." *Ellipse* 21 (1977): 105-107.

Reflections and ideas on the pleasures of translating poetry.

20. Claxton, Patricia. "Translation and Creation." *Actes du colloque: traduction et qualité de langue.* Société des traducteurs du Québec, 30-31 janvier/1er février, 1983. Hull, Québec: Éditeur officiel du Québec, 1984. 74-78.

Discusses the importance of translation for cross-cultural under-standing; gives a brief overview of translation history and problems; focusses on the quality and types of literary translation between French and English Canada; refers in particular to two translations of *Maria Chapdelaine* by Louis Hémon, and comments on the publication, in France, of the translation of Margaret Atwood's *Life before Man.*

21. Cloutier, Cécile. "Jongleries sur la traduction." *La Traduction: l'universitaire et le praticien.* Cahiers de traductologie, No 5. Édit. Arlette Thomas et Jacques Flamand. Congrès: Université du Québec à Montréal, 28-31 mai 1980. Ottawa: Éditions de l'Université d'Ottawa, 1984. 203-206.

Réfléchit sur la sensation procurée par le fait d'être traduit en anglais.

22. Cogswell, Fred. "In Praise of Translation/Éloge de la traduction." Trans. Monique Grandmangin. *Ellipse* 21 (1977): 92-97.

Response to D.G. Jones's "Grounds for Translation" [see 70]; discusses the similarity of their views, and then his own reasons for and problems in translating poetry, and how he believes trans-lating poems is a "sacred trust."

23. Cowan, Judith. "The Translation of Poetry." *Ellipse* 21 (1977): 102-104.

Discusses her experience and the special challenges in translating poetry.

24. Delisle, Jean. "Dans les coulisses de l'adaptation théâtrale." *Circuit* 12 (mars 1986): 3-8.

Examine les concepts d'adaptation et de traduction dans le théâtre québécois; parle de Michel Garneau et de sa solution, la tradaptation; cite Roch Carrier et Sheila Fischman à propos de traduction; décrit la table ronde sur l'adaptation au Salon du livre de l'Outaouais, 23 mars 1985.

25. Delisle, Jean. "Projet d'histoire de la traduction et de l'interprétation au Canada." *Histoire de la traduction au Canada*. Numéro spécial de *Meta* 2.1 (mars 1977): 66-77.

Décrit les éléments du projet: histoire des professions; production et traduction, phénomène d'acculturation; traite de la relation qui existe entre la traduction littéraire et le rôle de la traduction dans la société canadienne, et se demande si la traduction contribue à briser l'isolement des "deux solitudes."

26. Dimić, Milan. Voir 86.

27. Dostie, Gaëtan. Voir 86.

28. Downes, Gwladys V. "Is the Muse Bilingual?" *Meta* 14.4 (décembre 1969): 195-199.

Discusses "three styles of translation" of poetry: expressionistic, scrupulous respect for the syntax and language of the original, and the literal poetic. Gives examples of translating the poems of Yves Préfontaine, Rina Lasnier, Anne Hébert, André Major, and Alain Grandbois, and compares the act of translating to writing poetry.

29. Dudek, Louis and Michael Gnarowski. "Relations with French Writing in Canada." *The Making of Modern Poetry in Canada: Essential Articles on Contemporary Canadian Poetry in English*. Ed. Louis Dudek and Michael Gnarowski. Toronto: The Ryerson Press, 1967. 247-250.

Discusses the history of translation in both literatures; the recent improvement in quality and quantity, the need for more translations, especially of poetry, and for financial support within the context of English-French literary relations in Canada.

30. Dudek, Louis. "Parenté des littératures française et anglaise au Canada." Trad. Yves Lacroix. *Lettres et écritures* 1.2 (février 1964): 31-34.

Affirme que "la littérature des deux langues du Canada . . . [fait] partie d'une seule littérature"; nomme plusieurs poètes-traducteurs; commente le refus de Pamphile Le May de traduire le sens exact du roman de William Kirby, *Le Chien d'or*.

31. Ellenwood, [William] Ray. "The Automatic Translator." *Prism International* 20.3 (Spring 1982): 37-39.

Discussion of his translation of two poems by Claude Gauvreau, "The Shadow on the Hoop" and "Petrouchka," which appear in *Prism International* 20.3 (Spring 1982); points out the difficulties arising from Gauvreau's use of "exceptional" language, which combines linguistic structures and morphemes to create images.

32. Ellenwood, [William] Ray. "How Not to Quince Words." *Books in Canada* 5.5 (May 1976): 8-11.

Discusses the writings of Jacques Ferron, the man himself, and comments on a number of translations, particularly in relation to Ferron's penchant for old Canadian; gives examples from *Quince Jam*, *Wild Roses*, *The Juneberry Tree*, *The Saint-Elias* and *Tales from the Uncertain Country*.

33. Ellenwood, [William] Ray. "Literary Translation in Canada." *Academy of Canadian Writers Newsletter* 3.1 (October 1981): 5.

Discusses translating in Canada, the overall lack of good translations, the increase of translations in recent years, and the cultural benefit of translation.

34. Ellenwood, [William] Ray. "Some Actualities of Canadian Literary Translation." *Translation in Canadian Literature: Symposium 1982.* Reappraisals: Canadian Writers 9. Ed. Camille R. La Bossière. Ottawa: University of Ottawa Press, 1983. 61-72.

Presents facts and figures concerning the past and current situation of literary translation in Canada; establishes the need to translate more literary texts into the other language and for greater support by publishers; quotes Philip Stratford from his foreword to *Bibliography of Canadian Books in Translation/Bibliographie de livres canadiens traduits* [see 269]; mentions oddities of the publication of the translations of *Life before Man* by Margaret Atwood and *Canadians of Old* by Philippe Aubert de Gaspé.

35. Ellenwood, [William] Ray. "Some Notes on the Politics of Translation." *Atkinson Review of Canadian Studies* 2.1 (1984): 25-28.

Points out that translations are not listed among literary works under existing Canadian copyright legislation, discusses the politics of translation in John Glassco's *The Poetry of French Canada in Translation* and in Ralph Manheim's translation of Marie-Claire Blais's *St. Lawrence Blues*.

36. Ellenwood, William Ray. "Traduire le non-traduisible: faisant front à Claude Gauvreau." *La Traduction: l'universitaire et le praticien.*

Cahiers de traductologie, No 5. Édit. Arlette Thomas et Jacques Flamand. Congrès: Université du Québec à Montréal, 28-31 mai 1980. Ottawa: Éditions de l'Université d'Ottawa, 1984. 173-178.

Décrit les problèmes que lui a posés la traduction des aventures sémantiques qui émaillent la poésie automatique de Claude Gauvreau.

37. Ellenwood, [William] Ray. "Translating Nationalism—Jacques Ferron." Unpublished paper presented at Traduire la littérature du Québec/Translating Quebec Literature Conference, 9 mars 1984, Université Concordia.

Discussion of theoretical problems in taking Ferron's *Le Ciel de Québec*, which is so regionally and linguistically centred, and making it readable in English; refers to and draws examples from the *Dialogue* of Anne Hébert and Frank Scott [see 176], and Ralph Manheim's translation of Marie-Claire Blais's *Un Joualonais, sa joualonie* (*St. Lawrence Blues*).

38. Findlay, William. "Les Belles Sœurs (an extract)." Trans. Martin Bowman and William Findlay. *Cencratus* 3 (Summer 1980): 4-8.

Discusses the translation of *Les Belles Sœurs* into Scots; compares social and linguistic situation of Quebec and Scotland; sees Tremblay's use of *joual* as a useful model for Scotland.

39. Fischman, Sheila. "French and English Texts in Tandem: The Editing of *Ellipse*." *Editing Canadian Texts*. Papers given at the Conference on Editorial Problems, University of Toronto, 1972. Ed. Francess G. Halpenny. Toronto: A.M. Hakkert Ltd., 1975. 81-94.

Outlines the origins and practices of the translation journal *Ellipse*; lists numerous writers and translators who have been published in *Ellipse*; refers to John Glassco's *The Poetry of French Canada in Translation* and quotes from his introduction [see 227]; remarks on Glassco's work as a translator and Margaret Atwood's experimental translation of her own poetry.

40. Fischman, Sheila. See 65.

41. Follkart di Stefano, Barbara. "Translating as Literary Criticism." *Meta* 27.3 (septembre 1982): 241-256.

Discusses how "literary translation" is intrinsically an act of literary criticism, with reference to problems confronted by would-be translators of Sartre's *La Nausée* and Léonard Forest's preface "Le Pays de la Sagouine" in Antonine Maillet, *La Sagouine.*

42. Gauvin, Lise et Laurent Mailhot, édit. "Traductions." *Guide culturel du Québec.* Montréal: Boréal Express, 1982. 361-364.

Survol historique de la traduction au Canada.

43. Germain, Georges-Hébert. "Les Hauts et les bas de la vie littéraire." *L'Actualité* 8 (novembre 1983): 171-172.

Traite de l'histoire de la traduction de la littérature canadienne-anglaise en français et de l'indifférence manifestée par le lecteur québécois envers ces traducteurs.

44. Gerson, Carole. "Three Writers of Victorian Canada." *Canadian Writers and Their Works.* Fiction Series, Volume One. Ed. Robert Lecker, Jack David, and Ellen Quigley. Downsview, Ontario: ECW Press, 1983. 197-256.

Discussion of Rosanna Leprohon's works, which were translated during her own lifetime and were more popular in French translation than in English; refers in particular to *Antoinette de Mirecourt*, translated by J.A. Genand.

45. Giguère, Richard. "Quelques réflexions sur la traduction poétique au Québec et au Canada à partir du texte de J. Brault: 'Remarques sur la traduction de la poésie'/Some Reflections on the Translation of Poetry in Canada and Quebec, in reply to Jacques Brault's Paper." Trans. David Lobdell. *Ellipse* 21 (1977): 37-49.

Pose des questions à Brault au sujet de sa conception de la traduction et de la nontraduction, puis il brosse un tableau de l'état actuel de la traduction poétique au Canada et au Québec, et se demande pourquoi les Québécois ne traduisent pas; cite l'article de Philip Stratford paru dans *Meta* [voir 130] et sa préface dans *Bibliography of Canadian Books in Translation/Bibliographie de livres canadiens traduits* [voir 269]; mentionne l'article de John Glassco "The Opaque Medium" [voir 48]. Voir aussi 13; 86.

First responds to Brault's remarks on translation and non-translation, and second, gives a general picture of the present state of poetry translation in Canada and Quebec and discusses why there has been so little translation done in Quebec; cites Philip Stratford's article in *Meta* [see 130], and his foreword to *Bibliography of Canadian Books in Translation/Bibliographie de livres canadiens traduits* [see

269], and refers to John Glassco's article, "The Opaque Medium" [see 48]. See also 13; 86.

46. Giguère, Richard. "Traduction littéraire et 'image' de la littérature au Canada et au Québec." *Translation in Canadian Literature: Symposium 1982*. Reappraisals: Canadian Writers 9. Ed. Camille R. La Bossière. Ottawa: University of Ottawa Press, 1983. 47-60.

Historique et analyse de la traduction littéraire de tout genre au Canada: la poésie, le roman, le théâtre, l'essai; décrit la politique du Conseil des arts.

47. Giguère, Richard. "Translations: English to French." *The Oxford Companion to Canadian Literature*. Ed. William Toye. Toronto: Oxford University Press, 1983. 794-795.

Survey of stages of the translation of poetry, fiction, drama, and non-fiction from 1809, discussing numbers and types of texts translated and commenting on need for more translation of modern English-Canadian poetry. Claims that the "quality of literary translation has reached a respectable level over the past few years," and lists several successful translators; cites commentary from Philip Stratford's foreword to *Bibliography of Canadian Books in Translation* [see 269].

48. Glassco, John. "The Opaque Medium: Remarks on the Translation of Poetry with a Special Reference to French-Canadian Verse." *Meta* 14.1 (mars 1969): 27-30.

Comments on the history of translation of French-Canadian poetry before 1950 and on the opening up of the field (by F.R. Scott and others); points out problems and difficulties in translating poetry with examples from Peter Miller's translations of Alain Grandbois, Gaston Miron, Anne Hébert, and André Major.

49. Gnarowski, Michael. *The Extent and Condition of Canadian Literary Translation*. Royal Commission on Bilingualism and Biculturalism. Progress Report No. 1. Public Archives of Canada RG 33180. Vol. 83. 1967.

A study of the extent of the "translation of Canadian works of a literary/academic nature from French into English and vice versa" and of the role of "these translations as a means of cultural communication between the two major language groups of Canada"; makes specific recommendations.

50. Gnarowski, Michael. See 29.

51. Godard, Barbara. "Across Frontiers: Callaghan in French." *The Callaghan Symposium*. Reappraisals: Canadian Writers. Ed. David Staines. Ottawa: University of Ottawa Press, 1981. 47-58.

Discusses at length the art of translation and the role of the translator in transposing "a whole civilization" and the implications of this process for French and English Canada; refers to Anne Hébert and Saint-Denys Garneau; comments on the translation of English-Canadian texts and examines the cultural framework surrounding the few translations of Callaghan's novels: *Telle est ma bien-aimée* (*Such Is My Beloved*), *Cet été-là à Paris* (*That Summer in Paris*) and *Cette belle faim de vivre* (*A Passion in Rome*); the texts are analyzed in some detail in an attempt to determine what "cultural myths are generated" by these translations.

52. Godard, Barbara. "Language and Sexual Difference: The Case of Translation." *Atkinson Review of Canadian Studies* 2.1 (Fall/Winter 1984): 13-20. Also published with slight changes as "Translating and Sexual Difference" [see 53].

Discusses how sexual difference operates in all language acts including translation; gives examples from Québécois feminist writing and her translations of Nicole Brossard's *L'Amèr* and *Amantes* (*These Our Mothers* and *Lovhers*); compares her translation of Cécile Cloutier's poetry with that of Alexandre Amprimoz; and Linda Gaboriau's, David Ellis's, and Larry Shouldice's translations of Nicole Brossard's poetry; discusses Antonine Maillet's *Pélagie*, translated by Philip Stratford; gives examples from F.R. Scott's translation of Anne Hébert's "Le Tombeau des rois," and comments on *Dialogue sur la traduction* [see 176]; refers also to articles by Evelyne Voldeng [see 146] and Kathy Mezei [see 97].

53. Godard, Barbara. "Translating and Sexual Difference." *Resources for Feminist Research/Documentation sur la recherche féministe*. 13.3 (November 1984): 13-16. Rpt. with slight changes from "Language and Sexual Difference" [see 52].

Discusses how sexual difference operates in all language acts including translation; gives examples from Québécois feminist writing and her translations of Nicole Brossard's *L'Amèr* and *Amantes*.

54. Godard, Barbara. "The Translator as She: The Relationship between Writer and Translator." *in the feminine: women and words/les*

femmes et les mots. Conference Proceedings 1983. Ed. Ann Dybikowski, Victoria Freeman, Daphne Marlatt, Barbara Pulling, and Betsy Warland. Edmonton: Longspoon Press, 1985. 193-198.

Defines the act of translation and the "illicit pleasures of translating"; discusses her experience in translating women writers who "are consciously attempting to find new sources of meaning for women within language"; gives examples from her translation of Antonine Maillet's *Don l'Orignal* and Nicole Brossard's reaction to the translation of *L'Amèr*.

55.   Godard, Barbara. "The Translator as Ventriloquist." *Prism International* 20.3 (Spring 1982): 35-36. Rpt. in *Prism International*, 25th Anniversary issue, 23.2 (Winter 1984): 160-161.

Discusses her translation of "the temptation" (*Prism International* 20.3: 30-34) from Nicole Brossard's *Amantes*, pointing out her betrayal of the original in sacrificing meaning for sound.

56.   Gouin, Jacques. "La Traduction au Canada de 1791 à 1867." *Histoire de la traduction au Canada*. Numéro spécial de *Meta* 2.1 (mars 1977): 26-32.

Retrace brièvement l'histoire des traducteurs et interprètes canadiens-français professionnels parmi lesquels figurent Antoine Gérin-Lajoie, François-Xavier Garneau, Louis Fréchette et Pamphile Le May. Cite Joseph-Édouard Le Febvre de Bellefeuille qui a traduit les romans de Rosanna Leprohon.

57.   Grandpré, Chantal de. "La Canadianisation de la littérature québécoise: le cas Aquin." *Liberté* 149 (juin 1985): 50-59.

Traite des écrivains et des traducteurs canadiens qui essaient d'assimiler la littérature et la culture québécoises dans un contexte canadien-anglais; cite en exemples des traducteurs de Gaston Miron (Dennis Egan) et de Hubert Aquin (Penny Williams, Alan Brown et Sheila Fischman).

58.   Hancock, Geoff. "A Decade of Québec Fiction." *A Decade of Québec Fiction*. Special number of *Canadian Fiction Magazine* 47 (1984): 4-5.

Outlines the particular problems faced by literary translators in Canada: the work is too often "financially unrewarding," and press distribution inadequate; includes comments by several translators regarding the political and literary frameworks of translation.

59. Hancock, Geoff. "From a Certain Country." *Books in Canada* 11.2 (February 1982): 3-8.

A comprehensive discussion of translation in Canada; contrasts the literary forms of Québécois and English-Canadian writing; examines differences in French in terms of *joual*, narrative structure, kinds of narration and content, and the resulting difficulty faced by English translators of French texts; cites the views of translators Philip Stratford and Ray Ellenwood; refers to the translation of Anne Hébert's *The Torrent* and the writing of Jacques Ferron.

60. Hayne, David M. "*The Golden Dog* and *Le Chien d'or*, Le May's French Translation of Kirby's Novel." *Papers of the Bibliographical Society of Canada/Cahiers de la Société bibliographique du Canada* 20 (1981): 50-62.

Traces the publishing history of Pamphile Le May's French translation of Kirby's novel.

61. Hayne, David M. "Literary Translation in Nineteenth-Century Canada." *Translation in Canadian Literature: Symposium 1982*. Reappraisals: Canadian Writers 9. Ed. Camille R. La Bossière. Ottawa: University of Ottawa Press, 1983. 35-46.

Enumerates literary texts translated into both languages in order to describe the extent and variety of the translation of "belles-lettres," and discusses in detail the history of the French translation of William Kirby's *The Golden Dog*; concludes with a series of general observations on literary translation in the nineteenth century and states the need for a more detailed history.

62. Hébert, Anne and Frank Scott. "The Art of Translation." *The Tamarack Review* 24 (August 1962): 65-90. (The first English publication of the *Dialogue*) [see 176].

Includes three versions of the translation of "Le Tombeau des rois," a short note by Scott concerning the third version, and the Hébert-Scott correspondence.

63. Hébert, Anne et Frank Scott. "La Traduction: dialogue entre le traducteur et l'auteur." *Écrits du Canada français* 7 (1960): 193-236. (Première publication du *Dialogue*) [voir 176].

Deux versions de la traduction du "Tombeau des rois"; correspondance entre Scott et Hébert.

64. Hoffpauir, Richard. "A Response to D.G. Jones's 'Grounds for Translation.'" *Ellipse* 22 (1978): 107-113.

Responds to Jones's apparent misreading of his comments on Coleridge and divine frenzy (in relation to Emile Nelligan's poetry, to madness, and to translation), and attacks Jones's position which implies more interest in free than correct literary translation [see 70].

65. Homel, David [Toby]. "Solving the Difficulties: A Panel Discussion." *Translation Review* 20 (1986): 9-13.

Transcribed from the International Authors' Festival at Harbourfront in Toronto in October 1985. Sheila Fischman's comments on translating *joual* and Michel Tremblay's *The Fat Woman Next Door Is Pregnant* are of particular interest.

66. Homel, David [Toby]. "Le Traducteur dans la société; Canada/Québec." *Actes des deuxièmes assises de la traduction littéraire (Arles 1985)*. Arles, France: Actes Sud, 1986. 165-171.

Déclare qu'au Canada "traduire une œuvre littéraire revient à poser un geste politique"; décrit la situation de la traduction littéraire, la politique du Conseil des arts, les relations avec l'Union des écrivains du Québec, "les conditions dans lesquelles sont publiées les œuvres traduites du québécois en anglais à l'intention d'un public canadien-anglais"; déclare que, contrairement à l'opinion générale, il y a plus de textes québécois traduits en anglais que l'inverse; traite des problèmes que soulève la traduction d'une langue "dominée" vers une langue "dominante."

67. Homel, David [Toby]. "The Way They Talk in *Broke City*." *Translation Review* 18 (1985): 23-24.

Describes the characteristics and context of the Quebec dialect, *joual*, and his decision to translate *joual* in Jacques Renaud's *Broke City* by a "generalized, big-city, working-class, northern, white dialect."

68. Hutchison, Alexander. "On parole de battre et de vanner." *Ellipse* 29/30 (1982): 111-112.

Discusses the process of translating, his particular approach, the importance of sound and recreation of tone, and his goal that the translated work "*mean* and *resonate* and speak alive in some equivalent form."

69. Jones, D.G. "F.R. Scott as Translator." *On F.R. Scott*. Ed. Sandra Djwa and R. St. J. Macdonald. Kingston: McGill-Queen's University Press, 1983. 160-164.

Describes Scott's role as translator in opening a window on Quebec; comments on the quality of his translations of Hébert and Garneau, and compares them with Alan Brown's and John Glassco's.

70. Jones, D.G. "Grounds for Translation/Raisons d'être de la traduction." Trans. Joseph Bonenfant. *Ellipse* 21 (1977): 58-91. Rpt. in *The Insecurity of Art: Essays on Poetics*. Ed. Ken Norris and Peter Van Toorn. Montreal: Véhicule Press, 1982. 67-80.

Reflections on why one translates Quebec poetry into English and how both poems and translations aim at "effective communion"; mentions and quotes, but does not evaluate, the translations of numerous French-Canadian poets in order to demonstrate the thematic significance of the poetry and the value of its translation; comments at length on translations of the poetry of Emile Nelligan and refers to thematic differences between John Robert Colombo's *The Great Wall of China* and Jacques Godbout's translation, *La Grande Muraille de Chine*.

Remarques sur les raisons qui font traduire de la poésie québécoise en anglais et le fait que poèmes et traductions aspirent à une "communion efficace"; mentionne et cite, sans toutefois porter de jugement, les traductions de nombreux poèmes québécois de façon à démontrer l'importance thématique de la poésie et la valeur de sa traduction; commente longuement les traductions des poèmes d'Émile Nelligan; mentionne les différences thématiques qui existent entre *The Great Wall of China* de John Robert Colombo et *La Grande Muraille de Chine* de Jacques Godbout.

71. Jones, D.G. "Text and Context: Some Reflections on Translation with Examples from Quebec Poetry." Unpublished paper presented at Traduire la littérature au Québec/Translating Quebec Literature Conference, 9 mars 1984, Université Concordia.

Discusses the process of translating poetry and the necessity and difficulty of translating a poem's meaning into his own language, with examples from Pierre Nepveu, Anne Hébert, and David Homel's translation of *Broke City*, by Jacques Renaud.

72. Kattan, Naïm. "La Parole aux traducteurs: un travail sur sa propre langue." *Le Devoir* (samedi 22 février 1975): 15-16.

Traite du défi posé aux traducteurs et du rôle de ces derniers, particulièrement ceux qui ont traduit le Coran.

73. Kattan, Naïm. "Problèmes particuliers de la traduction de textes littéraires." *Translation and Interpretation: The Multicultural Con-*

text. A Symposium. Colloque sur le contexte multiculturel de la traduction et de l'interprétation. 18-19 April 1975, Université Carleton University, 18-19 avril 1975. Ed. and introduction by/éd. et introduction par Michael S. Batts. Vancouver: CAUTG: Canadian Association of University Teachers of German, 1975. 73-82.

Exemples de l'attitude envers la traduction de la part d'écrivains qui se sont engagés dans ce domaine: Shakespeare, la Bible, le Coran, "le nontraduire" de Jacques Brault [voir 174].

74. Kushner, Eva and Yves Merzisen. "D.G. Jones/Fred Cogswell (Discussion: Eva Kushner and Yves Merzisen)." *Ellipse* 21 (1977): 98-101.

Discussion of D.G. Jones, "Grounds for Translation" [see 70] and Fred Cogswell, "In Praise of Translation" [see 22].

75. La Bossière, Camille R. "Compass of the Catoptric Past: John Glassco, Translator." *Canadian Poetry* 13 (Fall/Winter 1983): 32-42.

A discussion of Glassco's views on the art of translation and the role of the translator, with reference to his introduction in *The Poetry of French Canada in Translation* [see 227]; substantial comparison and analysis of Glassco's translations, with examples from *Le Cœur en exil* (René Chopin), *Strophes et catastrophes* (François Hertel), *L'Homme et le jour* (Jean-Guy Pilon), *Les Fleurs boréales* (Louis-Honoré Fréchette), and the poetry of Octave Crémazie and Simone Routier.

76. La Fontaine, Gilles de. Voir 86.

77. Lang, George Maclean. "Témoignage." *Ellipse* 21 (1977): 108-110.

Description of his entry into translation, how every man is a translator, especially in Quebec, the richness of popular Quebec idiom; translation is "an artistic, visceral, even an intestinal act [and in] Québec it is also communal."

78. Lebel, Marc. "François-Xavier Garneau, traducteur." *Histoire de la traduction au Canada.* Numéro spécial de *Meta* 22.1 (mars 1977): 33-36.

Parle de Garneau en tant que traducteur à l'Assemblée législative du Canada-Uni de 1842 à 1844, de sa connaissance de la langue et de la littérature anglaise ainsi que de son insatisfaction vis-à-vis de la traduction de son *Histoire du Canada* par Andrew Bell.

79. Lemaire, Michel. "Jacques Brault dans le matin." *Voix et images* 2.2 (décembre 1976): 173-194.

Décrit le concept de nontraduction de Brault et son processus, le dialogue avec des poèmes des quatre auteurs anglo-saxons, "le travail du nontraducteur n'est pas de devenir l'autre (comme le désire le traducteur), mais de dépasser ces réalités limitées du moi et de l'autre, dans une fusion essentielle" [voir 174].

80. Levenson, Christopher. "Statement for a Panel Discussion." *Translation and Interpretation: The Multicultural Context. A Symposium.* Colloque sur le contexte multiculturel de la traduction et de l'interprétation. 18-19 April 1975, Université Carleton University, 18-19 avril 1975. Ed. Michael S. Batts. Vancouver: CAUTG: Canadian Association of University Teachers of German, 1975. 117-120.

Discussion of the role of the literary translator in a multi-cultural context and the importance of teaching translation.

81. Lotbinière-Harwood, Susanne de. "Les Belles Infidèles." *Arcade* 11 (février 1986): 22-25.

Traite de son "show de traduction" et de sa position en tant que traductrice féministe quand les traducteurs " 'seront'—selon le contexte—aussi infidèles que possible au bon usage (bon pour qui?) et à la loi du langage phallique."

82. Lotbinière-Harwood, Susanne de. "La Grammaire intérieure." *La Vie en rose* (septembre 1986): 34-35.

Traite de la relation qui existe entre la traduction, le langage et le féminisme. Mentionne la traduction qu'elle a faite de *La Terre est trop courte, Violette Leduc* de Jovette Marchessault.

83. Mailhot, Laurent, ed. Voir 42.

84. Manguel, Alberto. "Le Mot juste." *Saturday Night* 98.7 (July 1983): 53-54.

A detailed article about the translator Sheila Fischman: outlines her history as a translator; includes comments made by Fischman on the problems and difficulties of literary translation with examples from Anne Hébert's *Les Fous de Bassan*, and on her own "system for translating" and her "need to remain conscious of the difference" between the two languages; summarizes her theories of the criteria for good translation; outlines the publishing history and current situation, particularly economic, of translation in Canada.

85. Mantz, Douglas. "Acadjen, Eh? On Translating Acadian Literature." *Canadian Drama* 2.2 (Fall 1976): 188-195.

Discusses the importance of translating Acadian literature; presents a theory of how to translate Acadian (through "a composite maritime speech and slang"); detailed examination of Antonine Maillet's *La Sagouine*, including his translation of the play's opening scene.

86. Marcotte, Gilles et André Vanasse, Joseph Bonenfant, Milan Dimić, Gabrielle Poulin, Gilles de La Fontaine, Patricia Smart et Gaëtan Dostie. "J. Brault/R. Giguère." *Ellipse* 21 (1977): 50-57.

Réponse aux "Remarques sur la traduction de la poésie" de Jacques Brault [voir 13] et aux "Quelques réflexions sur la traduction poétique au Québec et au Canada, à partir du texte de J. Brault" de Richard Giguère [voir 45].

87. Marlatt, Daphne. "Notes." *Ellipse* 29/30 (1982): 84.

Three segments discussing what translation is, how it works, what is involved in the process, and the difficulties encountered by the translator; comments on the "semantic connection" between French and English, so that "translating in them can only be a spinning out of their relation."

88. Marshall, Joyce. "Gabrielle Roy 1909-1983, Some Reminiscences." *Canadian Literature* 101 (Summer 1984): 183-184.

Reflections on Roy's involvement with the translation of her writing, her concern that the specific meaning of the original be captured, and her unhappiness with the errors in *The Tin Flute*, translated by Hannah Josephson; discusses her own role as translator of Roy's work.

89. May, C.R.P. "Traduction, 'solitude rompue.'" *Ellipse* 21 (1977): 124-125.

Réflexions sur la traduction de la poésie: "mon intention dans la traduction est souvent didactique"—communiquer la poésie québécoise à d'autres.

90. McCaffery, Steve. "Agreement Between Favour and Desire." *Ellipse* 29/30 (1982): 120-126.

Discusses and analyzes the practice and process of translation, why translating is "so much foolishness."

91. McCaffery, Steve. "From the Unposted Correspondence." *Ellipse* 29/30 (1982): 44-45.

     Fragments of letters written while he was working on translations for *Ellipse* concerned with the "issues" of translation, his particular approach, and reflections on the process of translating.

92. McCaffery, Steve. "A Note on Translative Method." *Ellipse* 29/30 (1982): 142.

     Discusses the process of "topomorphic translation," whereby "the originary text" is passed "through an english 'filter' back into French"—"homolinguistic translation arrived at by passing through an anglographic mediate system."

93. McCormick, Marion. "Life in Translation." *Books in Canada* 6.8 (October 1977): 21-22.

     Account of Sheila Fischman's experience and practice as a translator of Québécois fiction; cites comments by Roch Carrier on being translated.

94. Merzisen, Yves. "La Mise en mots est une mise à mort." *Ellipse* 21 (1977): 120-123.

     Déclare que "la traduction poétique [n'est . . .] qu'une lecture plus attentive et plus poussée du poème"; compare le fait de traduire à la composition d'un poème; commente l'importance d'*Ellipse* qui établit un lien entre les deux littératures.

95. Merzisen, Yves. See 74.

96. Mezei, Kathy. "A Bridge of Sorts: The Translation of Quebec Literature into English." *Anglo-American Literary Relations*. Special number of *The Yearbook of English Studies* 15 (1985): 202-226.

     The history of literary translation from World War Two to the present and its significance in bridging the "two solitudes"; reflects on the role of *Ellipse*; mentions the role, theories, and influence of translators F.R. Scott, John Glassco, Philip Stratford, Louis Dudek, Peter Miller, and D.G. Jones; and reviews translations of Anne Hébert, Saint-Denys Garneau, Émile Nelligan, Alain Grandbois (*Selected Poems*), and Paul-Marie Lapointe (*The Terror of the Snows*).

97. Mezei, Kathy. "The Scales of Translation: The English-Canadian Poet as Literal Translator." *Revue de l'Université d'Ottawa/University of Ottawa Quarterly* 54.2 (April-June 1984): 63-84.

Discusses the factors determining whether a translation is literal, free, or faithful, and the relationship between poetry and translation; focusses on translations by F.R. Scott, John Glassco, D.G. Jones, Alan Brown, Barbara Godard, and Ray Ellenwood and the different degrees and significance of literalness; refers to: Jones's "Grounds for Translation" [see 70], the *Dialogue* of Anne Hébert and Frank Scott [see 176], *The Poetry of French Canada in Translation* [see 227], Gwladys Downes's *when we lie together* [see 213], and a number of other texts and translations.

98. Morley, William F.E. "Bibliographical Aspects of Bell's Translation of Garneau's *Histoire du Canada*." *Papers of the Bibliographical Society of Canada/Cahiers de la Société bibliographique du Canada* 28 (1979): 79-85.

Outlines the controversy over Andrew Bell's translation of François-Xavier Garneau's *Histoire du Canada, depuis sa découverte jusqu'à nos jours/History of Canada from the Time of its Discovery till the Union Year.*

99. Nepveu, Pierre. "Traduction/Écriture/Lecture." *Ellipse* 21 (1977): 118-119.

Décrit comment "la traduction a été pour moi une manière nouvelle de pratiquer et de vivre la poésie."

100. O'Connor, John. "Translations: French to English." *The Oxford Companion to Canadian Literature*. Ed. William Toye. Toronto: Oxford University Press, 1983. 795-798.

Documents the history of literary translation over three historical periods: 1. to 1959; 2. 1960-1971; 3. 1972-1981, with reference to the numbers and genres of texts translated; comments on the quality of specific translations, the variable expertise of certain translators, and on the rapid increase and "key landmarks" in translation activity up to 1978; emphasizes the importance of establishing high standards.

101. O'Hearn, Walter. "Too Deep for Tears or Mirth." *The Montreal Star* (10 March 1962) section Entertainments: 3.

Addresses the lack of translation in Canada at this time; claims that only Americans, but no English Canadians, had yet translated a French-Canadian novel; refers to the American translator of Canadian texts, Harry Lorin Binsse.

102. Ouellet, Réal. "Traduction ou création?" *Lettres québécoises* 23 (automne 1981): 60-61.

Traite de la traduction littéraire au Québec: compare la traduction et l'adaptation et traite surtout des traductions de textes anciens (non canadiens) par Jean Marcel; parle aussi de la situation au Canada.

103. Paquin, Robert. "Traduit au Québec: 'Les Succès des autres.'" *Spirale* 62 (été 1986): 14.

Décrit l'influence de la traduction sur la chanson québécoise.

104. Paratte, Henri-Dominique. "Discovering Two Literatures: Some Remarks About Translations of the Two Major Literatures of New Brunswick." *A Literary and Linguistic History of New Brunswick.* Ed. Reavley Gair. Fredericton: Fiddlehead Poetry Books and Goose Lane Editions, 1985.

Laments the lack of translations of Acadian literature into English; comments on the varying quality of the translations of Antonine Maillet by Luis de Céspedes, Barbara Godard, Wayne Grady, and Philip Stratford. Suggests the importance of carefully studying Acadian French and numerous dialects in English, and the desirability of more translation between the two cultures. Refers to Charles G.D. Roberts, Fred Cogswell, and Melvin Gallant as Maritime translators.

105. Paré, François. "*Maria Chapdelaine* au Canada anglais: réflexions sur notre extravagance." *Voix et images* 2.2 (décembre 1976): 265-278.

Avec pour contexte l'analyse de la réception réservée par le Canada anglais à *Maria Chapdelaine*, Paré traite de la traduction d'Andrew Macphail. Décrit en détail un article de Jacques Brierre qui n'a jamais été publié et déclare à tort que cet article compare les traductions de Blake et de Macphail [voir 15].

106. Paré, Jean. "La Parole aux traducteurs: 'Notes en marge de la traduction.'" *Le Devoir* 67.44 (samedi 22 février 1975): 15-16.

Compare le français et l'anglais; souligne les différences linguistiques et les conséquences pour les traducteurs littéraires.

107. Partensky, Jean-Paul. "La Situation du traducteur littéraire, l'expérience du Canada francophone." *Actes des deuxièmes assises de la traduction littéraire (Arles 1985)*. Arles, France: Actes Sud, 1986. 172-179.

Retrace brièvement l'histoire de la traduction au Canada, la politique du Conseil des arts; dresse la liste des auteurs canadiens-anglais traduits en français; parle de la fondation de l'Association des traducteurs littéraires et regrette les pratiques injustes de certains éditeurs.

108. Peraldi, François. "Traduit au Québec: 'Aux limites de la traduction: la psychanalyse.'" *Spirale* 62 (été 1986): 15.

Examine la question de la traduction du discours psychoanalytique.

109. Pivato, Joseph. "Writers in Translation." *Journal of Canadian Fiction* 3.2 (1974): 85-86.

Remarks on the cultural benefit of translating French-Canadian literature; describes the process of literary translation; raises numerous questions and concerns about a translator's technique and ability to understand and communicate the source text; cites critical commentary on the translation of classical literature as well as Canadian literature, in particular on *L'Incubation* by Gérard Bessette.

110. Plourde, Marc. "On Translating Miron: A Commentary." See 252.

111. Poulin, Gabrielle. Voir 86.

112. Reid, Malcolm. "Scaling the Language Barrier." *Quill & Quire* 42.7 (May 1976): 6-7, 9.

Focusses primarily on the question of translation in Canada, particularly the scarcity of books translated from English to French; suggests possible explanations.

113. Renaud, Gaston. "Translating Audrey Thomas Into French." *Translation Perspectives: Selected Papers, 1982-83*. Ed. Marilyn Gaddis Rose. Binghamton, New York: National Resource Center for Translation and Interpretation, Binghamton Site: SUNY-Binghamton Translation Research and Instruction Program, 1984.

With reference to a short story, "Spaghetti and Meatballs for Christmas," *Latakia*, and *Real Mothers*, discusses the difficulties of transposing culturally-bound source texts, which kind of French to use, and the difference between French expressions in France and Quebec.

114. Roberts, Roda P. "Evolution in Translation since 1966 as Reflected in the Pages of *Meta*." *Meta* 30.2 (juin 1985): 194-198.

Outlines the origins of the journal, its aims, and three main categories of changes: increased interest in writing about translation, the broadening scope, and changes in attitude towards specific aspects including machine translation and computers.

115. Schogt, Henry. "*Pas* lonely *pantoute?*" *Solitude rompue*. Cahiers du CRCCF. Édit. Cécile Cloutier-Wojciechowska et Réjean Robidoux. Ottawa: Éditions de l'Université d'Ottawa, 1986. 340-350.

Parle des problèmes concernant l'utilisation délibérée des régionalismes et la présence de l'anglais sous diverses formes pour la traduction de la prose, surtout la littérature canadienne écrite en français, et les solutions adoptées par W.H. Blake, Hannah Josephson, Sheila Fischman et Luis de Céspedes pour *Maria Chapdelaine* de Louis Hémon, *The Tin Flute* de Gabrielle Roy, *La Guerre, Yes Sir!* de Roch Carrier et *La Sagouine* d'Antonine Maillet.

116. Scott, Frank. See/voir 62; 63.

117. Shek, Ben-Zion. "Commentary on Antoine Sirois." Follows "Réception critique, au Québec, des romans en traduction de Mac-Lennan et rapports avec la production de l'autre solitude," by Antoine Sirois [see 125]. *Hugh MacLennan, 1982: Proceedings of the MacLennan Conference at University College*. Ed. Elspeth Cameron. Toronto: Canadian Studies Programme, University College, University of Toronto, 1983. 123-131.

Suggests that Sirois's statistical sampling of reviews is too small, that the reception of *Two Solitudes* in translation was more critical than Sirois suggests, and that few English-Canadian literary texts were being translated because of Quebec's perception of itself as a threatened culture.

118. Shek, Ben-Zion. "Quelques réflexions sur la traduction dans le contexte socio-culturel canado-québécois." *Ellipse* 21 (1977): 111-117. Also published in English translation: "Reflections on Translation: Canada and Quebec." *Comparison* 12 (Spring 1981): 32-40.

Étudie le rôle de la traduction, littéraire et autre, et sa contribution à la diglossie et au colonialisme au Québec, ainsi que l'importance et l'utilisation de l'anglais dans les romans québécois.

Discussion of the role of translation (public and literary) in contributing to diglossia and colonialism in Quebec, and the significance of the use of English in Quebec novels.

119. Shortliffe, Glen. "The Disease of Translation." *Meta* 14.1 (mars 1969): 22-26.

Discusses the perils of translation, its role in a bicultural country, and linguistic technicalities that create difficulties in translating French into English; gives illustrations from Gérard Bessette, *L'Incubation* et *Le Libraire*.

120. Shouldice, Larry. "Chacun son mishigos: The Translator as Comparatist." *Essays on Canadian Writing* 15 (Summer 1979): 25-32.

Compares the functions of translators and comparatists in a Canadian context, concluding that "the translator's activity is very akin to the comparatist's."

121. Shouldice, Larry. "On the Politics of Literary Translation in Canada." *Translation in Canadian Literature: Symposium 1982*. Reappraisals: Canadian Writers 9. Ed. Camille R. La Bossière. Ottawa: University of Ottawa Press, 1983. 73-82.

Comments on the Literary Translators' Association and the Canada Council; outlines political and literary reasons for the translation of certain texts and their style, with specific references to translators: D.G. Jones, Sheila Fischman, Monique Grandmangin, Judith Cowan, David Lobdell, Michelle Tisseyre, and Michelle Robinson; to writers: Claire Martin, Gaston Miron, Gabrielle Roy, Michèle Lalonde, and Pierre Vallières; and to translations: *The Tin Flute* and *White Niggers of America*.

122. Simon, Sherry. "Traduit au Québec: 'Des produits de chez nous?'" *Spirale* 62 (été 1986): 11.

Traite de la signification de la traduction "le *cumul des choix*" et "la *manière* de traduire," et de la situation de la traduction de la littérature canadienne-anglaise en français.

123. Simon, Sherry. "Traduit au Québec: 'Se voir comme dans un miroir.'" *Spirale* 62 (été 1986): 14-15.

Survol historique des traductions du français à l'anglais et des nouvelles re-traductions ainsi que des problèmes qui se posent pour trouver l'équivalent du franco-québécois.

124.   Sirois, Antoine. "Gabrielle Roy et le Canada anglais." *Études littéraires* 17.3 (hiver 1984): 469-479.

Signale la réception favorable réservée par les critiques au *Bonheur d'occasion* de Gabrielle Roy et à sa traduction *The Tin Flute* de Hannah Josephson.

125.   Sirois, Antoine. "Réception critique, au Québec, des romans en traduction de MacLennan et rapports avec la production de l'autre solitude." *Hugh MacLennan, 1982: Proceedings of the MacLennan Conference at University College.* Ed. Elspeth Cameron. Toronto: Canadian Studies Programme, University College, University of Toronto, 1983. 114-122. Suivi d'un commentaire de Ben-Zion Shek, 123-131 [voir 117].

Décrit la réception critique exceptionnelle accordée aux traductions *Les Deux solitudes* (par Louise Gareau Des Bois), *Le Temps tournera au beau* (par Jean Simard), *Le Matin d'une longue nuit* (par Jean Simard); suggère qu'il y avait une attitude plus réceptive face au Canada anglais dans les années d'après-guerre.

126.   Smart, Patricia. Voir 86.

127.   Stainsby, Mari. "A Paraphrase of the Vision: French-Canadian Writing in Translation." *The British Columbia Library Quarterly* 26 (22 January 1963): 3-10.

Begins with an overview of the translation industry in Canada; discusses the lack of good translation in terms of the relationship between French and English Canadians; refers to a number of French-Canadian writers who have been translated, but includes no evaluation of the translations; claims that translation is valuable to increased cultural understanding; lists a number of French and English writers who had or had not been translated (most of whom have since been translated).

128.   Stratford, Philip. "The Anatomy of a Translation: *Pélagie-la-Char-rette*." *Translation in Canadian Literature: Symposium 1982.* Reappraisals: Canadian Writers 9. Ed. Camille R. La Bossière. Ottawa: University of Ottawa Press, 1983. 121-130.

Describes the "empirical principles, devices, and routines" of the process of translating Antonine Maillet's *Pélagie-la-Charrette*, and finding a suitable language for the translation of Acadian; also describes the role of a literary translator and the situation of literary translation in Canada.

129.   Stratford, Philip. "A bridge between two solitudes." *Language and Society* 11 (Autumn 1983): 8-13.

Examines literary translation in Canada; begins with an historical overview, continues with a look at current trends in the number of translations in Canada; comments on the role of translation as a "bridge" between the two dominant cultures in Canada, and discusses "the profession and its future"; includes an original and translated version of Anne Hébert's poem, "Le Tombeau des rois"/"The Tomb of Kings."

130.   Stratford, Philip. "French-Canadian Literature in Translation" with "Selected Bibliography." *Meta* 13.4 (décembre 1969): 180-187.

A survey of French-Canadian literature in translation: remarks on the scarcity of English novels in French translation; outlines the state of publishing and the role of the Canada Council in funding literary translations; comments on the cultural role of translation; suggests that the educational system could be used to make translation a "household" word; includes a selected bibliography of literary translations from French to English.

131.   Stratford, Philip. "Literary Translation in Canada: A Survey." *Histoire de la traduction au Canada*. Numéro spécial de *Meta* 22.1 (mars 1977): 37-44. Also published as Foreword. *Bibliography of Canadian Books in Translation: French to English and English to French/Bibliographie de livres canadiens traduits de l'anglais au français et du français à l'anglais*. By Philip Stratford. Second Edition. Ottawa: HRCC/CCRH, 1977. i-viii; French translation as Préface. ix-xvii.

An overview of the state of translation of literature in Canada, beginning with the first published translations in the nineteenth century and including current programmes to encourage future projects.

Une vue d'ensemble de l'état de la traduction de la littérature au Canada, depuis la publication des premières œuvres traduites au XIXᵉ siècle jusqu'aux programmes actuels d'aide aux projets de traduction.

132.   Stratford, Philip. "Quebec Writers and Translators Meet." *Quill & Quire* 45.14 (December 1979): 14.

An outline of the discussion held by French-Canadian writers and English translators at a meeting of the representatives of the Union des Écrivains québécois and members of the Literary Translators' Association/Association des Traducteurs littéraires; includes references to the comments made by writers and translators (Michel Beaulieu, Nicole Brossard, Joyce Marshall, André Major, and Jacques Ferron) on the processes and difficulties of translation, the "right of the translator" and the need for increased translation in Canada; also includes a summary of comments made by "French-philosopher critic" Jacques Derrida at a meeting on translation at l'Université de Montréal.

133.   Stratford, Philip. "Reconciling the two solitudes." *Quill & Quire* 45.13 (November 1979): 12, 14.

Discusses state of translation in both languages, with suggestions for increasing the profile of translation in Canada; refers to Hannah Josephson's translation of Gabrielle Roy's *Bonheur d'occasion* (*The Tin Flute*) and cites the activities and opinions of Pierre Tisseyre, a publisher of French translations of English-Canadian texts.

134.   Stratford, Philip. "Translation as Creation." *Figures in a Ground: Canadian Essays on Modern Literature Collected in Honor of Sheila Watson*. Ed. Diane Bessai and David Jackel. Saskatoon: Western Producer Prairie Books, 1978. 9-18.

Uses colourful images to describe the translator and the act of translating; describes the process of translating, outlining his theories and the relation between source and target text; draws analogies and parallels between translator and writer.

135.   Stratford, Philip. "Translations." *The Oxford Companion to Canadian History and Literature. Supplement*. Ed. William Toye. Toronto: Oxford University Press, 1973. 302-303.

Outline of history of literary translation from French to English and English to French from 1863 to 1970; discusses paucity of translations and the quality of translations including Charles G.D. Roberts's *Canadians of Old* (by Philippe Aubert de Gaspé), *Christmas in French Canada* (by Louis Fréchette), Joyce Marshall's *Word from New France* (by Marie de l'Incarnation), *The Road Past Altamont* and *Windflower* (by Gabrielle Roy). Comments on certain poet-translators—F.R. Scott (*St.-Denys Garneau and*

Anne Hébert, and *Dialogue sur la traduction*); Fred Cogswell (*One Hundred Poems of Modern Quebec*; *A Second Hundred Poems of Modern Quebec*); John Glassco (*The Journal of Saint-Denys Garneau, The Poetry of French Canada in Translation*); on mistranslations and difficulties in Hannah Josephson's *The Tin Flute* (by Gabrielle Roy); Gérald Robitaille's *Flat Broke and Beat* (by Jacques Renaud); and Alan Brown's *Hail Galarneau!* (by Jacques Godbout). Lists Canadian periodicals that publish translations, bibliographies, and a small number of English-Canadian works in translation.

136. Stuewe, Paul. "Exploring a Labyrinth of Tongues: From the Folklore of Quebec to a Trenchant Analysis of Soviet Society." *Books in Canada* 10.8 (October 1981): 28-31.

Introduction to a new column, "In Translation"; summarizes the column's establishment and its purpose.

137. Surridge, Marie. "Le Rôle du genre grammatical dans la cohésion textuelle; un problème technique de la traduction du français vers l'anglais." *La Traduction: l'universitaire et le praticien*. Cahiers de traductologie, No 5. Édit. Arlette Thomas et Jacques Flamand. Congrès: Université du Québec à Montréal, 28-31 mai 1980. Ottawa: Éditions de l'Université d'Ottawa, 1984. 160-172.

Le genre grammatical intéresse effectivement la stylistique comparée et le traducteur; les exemples sont *Du côté de chez Swann* de Proust, *L'Être et le néant* de Sartre et *La Montagne secrète* de Gabrielle Roy.

138. Sutherland, Fraser. "John Glassco: An Essay." *John Glassco: An Essay and Bibliography*. Downsview, Ontario: ECW Press, 1984. 7-45.

Includes a discussion and summary of Glassco's ideas about the practice of translation (fidelity not literalness; translation as a bridge between two cultures); discusses Glassco's excellence as a translator and the works he translated (pp. 40-42).

139. Sutherland, Fraser. "Survey: In Other Words . . . " *Books in Canada* 15.1 (January/February 1986): 12-15.

Discussion by several Canadian literary translators about works they think should be translated; the translators of Québec literature included are: Sheila Fischman, Philip Stratford, Mark Czarnecki,

Betty Bednarski, Michael Bullock, Ray Ellenwood, Kathy Mezei, Ronald Sutherland, and Larry Shouldice.

140. Sutherland, Ronald. "The Literature of Quebec in Translation." *Read Canadian: A Book about Canadian Books*. Ed. Robert Fulford, David Godfrey, and Abraham Rotstein. Toronto: James Lewis and Samuel, 1972. 237-245.

Describes translation as a necessity, compares availability of French and English translations in Canada; outlines plot summaries and themes of major Quebec novels in translation; lists anthologies of Quebec poets in translation, and bibliographies—his in *Second Image* [see 172] and Philip Stratford's in *Meta* [see 130].

141. Sutherland, Ronald. "Notes on Translation and Comparative Studies in Canada." *Second Image: Comparative Studies in Quebec/ Canadian Literature*. By Ronald Sutherland. Toronto: New Press, 1971. 157-165.

Description of literary translations from the nineteenth century to time of publication, studies of French- and English-Canadian literature written in the other language, and of articles and books comparing the two literatures.

142. Thaon, Brenda. "Michel Garneau's *Macbeth*: An Experiment in Translating." *La Traduction: l'universitaire et le praticien*. Cahiers de traductologie, No 5. Édit. Arlette Thomas et Jacques Flamand. Congrès: Université du Québec à Montréal, 28-31 mai 1980. Ottawa: Éditions de l'Université d'Ottawa, 1984. 207-212.

Describes the translation and adaptation of *Macbeth* into a "québécois classique."

143. Tisseyre, Pierre. "Le Point de vue de l'éditeur." *Meta* 14.1 (mars 1969): 31-33.

Aborde les problèmes pratiques que rencontre l'éditeur de traductions littéraires, tels que les subventions du Conseil des arts, les rémunérations élevées qu'exigent de bons traducteurs, la définition d'un bon traducteur.

144. Van Toorn, Peter. "The Pain Called Babel." *Antigonish Review* 53 (Spring 1983): 99-107.

Claims that "all imaginative use of language involves translation if by translation you mean reciprocation"; discusses how translating is "the job of fitting square signs into round symbols," particularly in the translation of poetry; comments on the translator's personal involvement with a text; reflects on the experience of translating, the desire to be faithful to tone and intent, and the process and difficulties involved.

145. Vanasse, André. Voir 86.

146. Voldeng, Evelyne. "La Traduction poétique: duplication ou dérivation textuelle d'une langue à une autre?" *La Traduction: l'universitaire et le praticien*. Cahiers de traductologie, No 5. Édit. Arlette Thomas et Jacques Flamand. Congrès: Université du Québec à Montréal, 28-31 mai 1980. Ottawa: Éditions de l'Université d'Ottawa, 1984. 150-159. Paru aussi dans *Meta* 29.2 (juin 1984): 220-224.

Se demande dans quelle mesure la traduction en langue d'arrivée est fonction du genre du texte poétique traduit et du traducteur, avec des exemples tirés de Nicole Brossard (traduite par D.G. Jones, Linda Gaboriau), André Major (traduit par Gwladys Downes), Émile Nelligan (traduit par Sinclair Robinson, George Johnston), Cécile Cloutier (traduite par Barbara Godard, Alexandre Amprimoz) [voir 147].

147. Voldeng, Evelyne. "Trans Lata/Trans Latus." Trans. Frances Morgan. *TESSERA*. Special number of *Room of One's Own* 8.4 (1984): 82-96.

Parle longuement d'une section: "La Traduction poétique" [voir 146], s'intéressant surtout aux textes féministes traduits par des féministes et des traducteurs de sexe masculin en s'appuyant sur des exemples tirés de Cécile Cloutier (traduite par Barbara Godard et Alexandre Amprimoz), Nicole Brossard (traduite par Linda Gaboriau et David Ellis) et Sylvia Plath (traduite par Laure Vernière et Sinclair Robinson).

Expanded excerpt of "La Traduction poétique" [see 146], focussing on the comparison of feminist texts translated by feminists and male translators, with examples drawn from Cécile Cloutier (trans. Barbara Godard and Alexandre Amprimoz), Nicole Brossard (trans. Linda Gaboriau and David Ellis), and Sylvia Plath (trans. Laure Vernière and Sinclair Robinson).

148. Warwick, Jack. "Le Dilemme du traducteur d'œuvres anciennes." *La Traduction: l'universitaire et le praticien*. Cahiers de traduc-

tologie, No 5. Édit. Arlette Thomas et Jacques Flamand. Congrès: Université du Québec à Montréal, 28-31 mai 1980. Ottawa: Éditions de l'Université d'Ottawa, 1984. 141-149.

Étudie les problèmes que pose la traduction des récits de voyages, s'appuyant sur des exemples tirés de *L'Histoire du Canada* (1636) et du *Grand voyage* (1632) de Gabriel Sagard.

149. Whiteman, Bruce. "The Publication of *Maria Chapdelaine* in English." *Papers of the Bibliographical Society of Canada/Cahiers de la Société bibliographique du Canada* 21 (1982): 52-59.

Outlines the history of the different translations of *Maria Chapdelaine*.

150. Wilson, Paul. "Keepers of the Looking-Glass: Some Thoughts on Translation." *Brick: A Journal of Reviews* 26 (Winter 1986): 34-37.

Reflections on the art and processes of translation.

151. Agence littéraire des Canadiens français. *Titres canadiens-français traduits au Canada et/ou traduits et publiés à l'étranger.* Montréal: Conseil supérieur du livre, 1969. (Édition revue et augmentée, 1971. Polycopiée).

152. Albert, Lorraine et Jean Delisle. *Répertoire bibliographique de la traduction/Bibliographic Guide to Translation.* Compilé à l'intention des étudiants de l'École de traducteurs et d'interprètes de l'Université d'Ottawa/Prepared for Students of the School of Translators and Interpreters at the University of Ottawa. Ottawa: Morisset Library, Université d'Ottawa/University of Ottawa, 1976.

Avec commentaires/with annotations.

153. "Annual Bibliography of Commonwealth Literature: Canada." *Journal of Commonwealth Literature.*

1964 in Sept. 1965; 1: 27-43.	Compiled by Carl F. Klinck.
1965 in Dec. 1966; 2: 39-55.	Compiled by Carl F. Klinck.
1966 in Dec. 1967; 4: 46-62.	Compiled by Mary M.S. Brown.
1967 in Jan. 1969; 6: 43-63.	Compiled by Mary M.S. Brown.
1968 in Dec. 1969; 8: 89-106.	Compiled by Robert Weaver.
1969 in Dec. 1970; 10: 51-79.	Compiled by William H. New.
1970 in Dec. 1971; 6.2: 43-67.	Compiled by Mary Burnett.
1971 in Dec. 1972; 7.2: 59-86.	Compiled by William H. New.
1972 in Dec. 1973; 8.2: 59-97.	Compiled by W.H. New.
1973 in Dec. 1974; 9.2: 54-94.	Compiled by W.H. New.
1974 in Dec. 1975; 10.2: 72-107.	Compiled by W.H. New.
1975 in Part 1, Dec. 1976; 11.2: 30-81.	Compiled by W.H. New.
1976 in Part 1, Dec. 1977; 12.2: 24-84.	Compiled by W.H. New.
1977 in Part 1, Dec. 1978; 13.2: 51-110.	
1978 in Dec. 1979; 14.2: 42-86.	Compiled by Marilyn G. Flitton.
1979 in Dec. 1980; 15.2: 59-86.	Compiled by Doreen Ingram.
1980 in Feb. 1982; 16.2: 52-79.	Compiled by Moshie Dahms. Introduction by W.H. New.
1981 in 1982; 17.2: 52-84.	Compiled by Moshie Dahms. Introduction by W.H. New.

1982 in 1983; 18.2: 54-91.	Compiled by Moshie Dahms. Introduction by W.H. New.
1983 in 1984; 19.2: 44-78.	Compiled by Moshie Dahms. Introduction by W.H. New.
1984 in 1985; 20.2: 42-81.	Compiled by Moshie Dahms. Introduction by W.H. New.
1985 in 1986; 21.2: 42-79.	Compiled by Moshie Dahms. Introduction by W.H. New.

Lists translations in 11.2 (December 1976); comments on the quality of the translation of Gabrielle Roy's *The Road Past Altamont* (by Joyce Marshall), Rodolphe Girard's *Marie Calumet* (by Irène Currie), Félix-Antoine Savard's *Master of the River* (by Richard Howard), Naïm Kattan's *Farewell, Babylon* (by Sheila Fischman), Nicole Brossard's *Turn of a Pang* (by Patricia Claxton) in 12.2 (December 1977); lists translations in 13.2 (December 1978); 15.2 (December 1980); 16.2 (February 1982); and 17.2 (1982).

154. Cotnam, Jacques. "French-Canadian Literature in Translation." *Contemporary Quebec: An Analytical Bibliography*. Toronto: McClelland and Stewart, 1973. 72-76.

   List of primary sources translated into English from 1950 to 1971, with title of source text following in parentheses.

155. Crane, Nancy. See 167.

156. Delisle, Jean et Lorraine Albert. Compilé par/Compiled by. *Guide bibliographique du traducteur, rédacteur et terminologue/Bibliographic Guide for Translators, Writers and Terminologists*. Cahiers de traductologie, No 1. Ottawa: Éditions de l'Université d'Ottawa/ University of Ottawa Press, 1979.

   Édition revue, corrigée et augmentée de plus de 500 titres du *Répertoire bibliographique de la traduction* et qui s'adresse à un public élargi, et non plus aux seuls étudiants de l'Université d'Ottawa [voir 152].

   A revised edition of the *Bibliographic Guide to Translation*, updated to include over 500 new titles, intended for a wider readership than the students at the University of Ottawa [see 152].

157. Delisle, Jean. Voir/see 152.

158. Godard, Barbara. "Francophone Canada." *Women Writers in Translation: An Annotated Bibliography, 1945-1981*. Ed. Margery Resnick and Isabelle de Courtivron. Boston: Garland, 1984. 93-112.

This annotated bibliography includes an introduction to the history and state of the translation of francophone women writers in Quebec, as well as short descriptions of texts and brief evaluations of the translations.

159. Hayne, David M. and Antoine Sirois. "Preliminary Bibliography of Comparative Canadian Literature (English-Canadian and French-Canadian)." *Canadian Review of Comparative Literature/Revue canadienne de littérature comparée.* 3.2 (Spring 1976): 124-136.
Second Supplement, 1976-77. 5.1 (Winter 1978): 114-119.
Third Supplement, 1977-78. 6.1 (Winter 1979): 75-81.
Fourth Supplement, 1978-79. 7.1 (Winter 1980): 93-98.
Fifth Supplement, 1979-80. 8.1 (Winter 1981): 93-98.
Sixth Supplement, 1980-81. 9.2 (June 1982): 235-240.
Seventh Supplement, 1981-82. 10.1 (March 1983): 80-85.
Eighth Supplement, 1982-83. 11.1 (March 1984): 84-90.
and Jean Vigneault, Ninth Supplement, 1983-84. 12.3 (September 1985): 462-468.
Tenth Supplement, 1984-85. 13.3 (September 1986): 450-457.

Includes: Division 12, Literary Translation (English-Canadian and French-Canadian Literature);
12.1 Bibliographies of Translations;
12.2 Anthologies of Translations;
12.3 Theory of Literary Translation in Canada;
12.4 English Translations with Introductions or Commentaries;
12.5 French Translations with Introductions or Commentaries;
12.6 Criticism of Translation.

160. Jain, Sushil K. "French-Canadian Literature in English." *Canadian Author and Bookman* 40.4 (Summer 1965): 19.

Brief list of works in translation (completed in next issue) compiled from catalogues of Regina Campus Library of University of Saskatchewan. Includes plot summary, descriptions quoted from introductions, forewords, etc. [see 161].

161. Jain, Sushil K. "French-Canadian Literature in English." *Canadian Author and Bookman* 41.1 (Autumn 1965): 12-13.

Brief list of works in translation (concluded from last issue) compiled from catalogues of Regina Campus Library of University of Saskatchewan. Includes plot summary, descriptions quoted from introductions, forewords, etc. [see 160].

162. Leland, Marine. Revised by John Hare. "French Literature of Canada." Part 2: French Literature. *The Romance Literatures* Vol. 3. *The Literatures of the World in English Translation: A Bibliography*. Ed. George B. Parks and Ruth Z. Temple. New York: Ungar, 1970. 576-590.

     Selected list of bibliographies, literary studies, and major authors in English translation, with some descriptive annotations.

163. National Library of Canada/Bibliothèque nationale du Canada. *Canadian Translations/Traductions canadiennes 1984-1985*. Ottawa: National Library of Canada/Bibliothèque nationale du Canada, 1987.

     Includes a section of translated literary works.

     Comprend une section de traductions littéraires.

164. Newman, Maureen. See 169.

165. Quebec Work Group. *Quebec Literature in Translation: A Resource Guide for the Teaching of Canadian Literature*. Toronto: The Writers' Development Trust, 1977.

     Annotated list of Novels, Short Stories, Poetry, Drama, Non-Fiction in translation; only a few annotations refer to the quality of the translation.

166. Sanderson, David H. "Bibliographie." *Texte* 4 (1985): 253-312.

     Bibliographie détaillée sur la traduction; comprend la théorie, la traduction et le texte, l'histoire, des sources, des textes et des auteurs canadiens.

167. Senécal, André and Nancy Crane. *Quebec Studies: A Selected Annotated Bibliography*. Burlington, Vermont: Information Center on Canada, 1982.

     Lists translations into English in section "Literature Written in French," (pp. 88-135).

168. Sirois, Antoine. See 159.

169. Stratford, Philip and Maureen Newman. *Bibliography of Canadian Books in Translation: French to English and English to French/ Bibliographie de livres canadiens traduits de l'anglais au français et du français à l'anglais*. Prepared for the Committee on Translation of the Humanities Research Council of Canada/préparé pour

le Comité de la traduction du Conseil canadien de recherches sur les humanités. Ottawa: Humanities Research Council of Canada/ Conseil canadien de recherches sur les humanités, 1975. Stratford, Philip. Second edition/deuxième édition. Ottawa: HRCC/CCRH, 1977.

170. Stratford, Philip. " 'Selected Bibliography,' French-Canadian Literature in Translation" [see 130].

171. Sutherland, Fraser. "John Glassco: A Bibliography: 'Translations.' " *John Glassco: An Essay and Bibliography*. Downsview, Ontario: ECW Press, 1984. 75-77.

Lists translations published in journals, his poetry collections, and *The Poetry of French Canada in Translation*.

172. Sutherland, Ronald. "Bibliography: French-Canadian Fiction in English Translation; English-Canadian Fiction in French Translation." *Second Image: Comparative Studies in Quebec/Canadian Literature*. By Ronald Sutherland. Toronto: New Press, 1971. 178-181.

173. Sutherland, Ronald. "Bibliography: Quebec Fiction in English Translation." *The New Hero: Essays in Comparative Quebec/Canadian Literature*. By Ronald Sutherland. Toronto: Macmillan, 1977. 110-112.

174. Brault, Jacques. *Poèmes des quatre côtés*. Saint-Lambert: Éditions du Noroît, 1975.

Ce texte est divisé en quatre côtés comprenant des nontraductions de John Haines, Gwendolyn MacEwen, Margaret Atwood et e.e. cummings ainsi qu'une réflexion portant sur la poésie, la langue et la technique de nontraduction pratiquée par Brault. C'est un procédé qui se définit par des concepts contraires ("traduire, mais sans traduire," "nontraduire, c'est la fidélité qui aspire à l'infidélité") et qui, par son va-et-vient entre le texte de départ et celui d'arrivée et son refus de favoriser l'un d'eux, permet à tous deux de conserver leur essence et leur liberté et crée ainsi un "intertexte."

175. Flamand, Jacques. Voir 183.

176. Hébert, Anne et Frank Scott. *Dialogue sur la traduction à propos du "Tombeau des rois."* Montréal: Éditions HMH, 1970.

Comprend trois versions de traduction du poème d'Hébert par Scott, ainsi qu'une note explicative de Scott, la correspondance échangée entre Hébert et Scott, une préface de Northrop Frye (traduite par Jean Simard) [voir 221] et de Jeanne Lapointe.

177. La Bossière, Camille R., ed. *Translation in Canadian Literature: Symposium 1982*. Reappraisals: Canadian Writers 9. Ed. and with an introduction by Camille R. La Bossière. Ottawa: University of Ottawa Press, 1983.

A collection of essays on literary translation in Canada; essays on translation from French to English or English to French by E.D. Blodgett, Ray Ellenwood, Richard Giguère, David M. Hayne, Larry Shouldice, and Philip Stratford [see 8; 34; 46; 61; 121; 128].

178. Norris, Ken and Peter Van Toorn, eds. *The Insecurity of Art: Essays on Poetics*. Montreal: Véhicule Press, 1982.

Contains: Jones, D.G. "Grounds for Translation" [see 70]; Plourde, Marc, "On Translating Miron" [see 252]; Scott, F.R. Preface to *Poems of French Canada* [see 258].

179. Scott, Frank. Voir 176.

180. Sotiropoulou-Papaleonidas, Irène. *Jacques Brault: théories/pratique de la traduction; nouvelle approche de la problématique de la traduction poétique*. Sherbrooke: Éditions Didon, 1981.

Retrace le développement des théories sur la traduction poétique depuis les années 50; décrit la poésie de Jacques Brault et sa critique; traite des théories de Brault sur la traduction de la poésie—la nontraduction, "fruit d'un désir de communication-communion, toujours en suspens et toujours suspendu entre deux textes, sorte d'inter-texte . . . qui met sur un pied d'égalité l'auteur et le traducteur"; compare en détail les poèmes de départ et les traductions, notamment différentes versions de traduction des *Poèmes des quatre côtés*; fait un bref rappel historique de la traduction au Canada [voir 174].

181. Stratford, Philip. *Marie-Claire Blais*. Ed. William French. Canadian Writers and Their Works. Toronto: Forum House Publishing, 1971.

A few brief comments on the translations; in particular, p. 64, footnote 1, refers to the absence of the last 18 pages in *Vivre! Vivre!* (*The Manuscripts of Pauline Archange*) translated by Derek Coltman, who has otherwise produced a faithful and imaginative rendition of the original.

182. Sutherland, Fraser. *John Glassco: An Essay and Bibliography*. Downsview, Ontario: ECW Press, 1984 [see 138; 171].

183. Thomas, Arlette et Jacques Flamand, édit. *La Traduction: l'universitaire et le praticien*. Cahiers de traductologie, No 5. Congrès: Université du Québec à Montréal, 28-31 mai 1980. Ottawa: Éditions de l'Université d'Ottawa, 1984.

Comprend les rapports d'activité de deux ateliers qui traitaient de la traduction littéraire; avec des présentations de Alexandre Amprimoz, Cécile Cloutier, Ray Ellenwood, Marie Surridge, Brenda Thaon et Evelyne Voldeng dans un contexte canadien [voir 1; 21; 36; 137; 142; 146].

184. *Traduire notre poésie/The Translation of Poetry*. Transactions of a joint colloquium of ACQL/ALCQ and CCLA/ACLA, Fredericton, May 1977. Special number of *Ellipse* 21 (1977).

Comprend des articles écrits par/includes articles by Jacques Brault, Léo-A. Brodeur, Fred Cogswell, Judith Cowan, Richard Giguère, D.G. Jones, George Maclean Lang, C.R.P. May, Yves Merzisen, Pierre Nepveu et/and Ben-Zion Shek [voir/see 13; 19; 22; 23; 45; 70; 77; 89; 94; 99; 118].

185. Usmiani, Renate. *Gratien Gélinas*. Profiles in Canadian Drama. Toronto: Gage Educational Publishing, 1977.

Points out difficulties of translating popular idiom; claims that the translation of *Tit-Coq* (Kenneth Johnstone) is pale compared to the original. The translation of *Bousille and the Just* (Kenneth Johnstone and Joffre Miville-Dechêne) is superior; although it too has certain problems with idiom, it is structurally an improvement over the French. The translation of *Yesterday the Children Were Dancing* (Mavor Moore) does "full justice to the original," partly due to a more universal and easily transposed context.

186. Usmiani, Renate. *Michel Tremblay*. Vancouver: Douglas and MacIntyre, 1982.

Chapter Two, "Contexts of the Tremblay Opus," includes a section on the "problems of translation"; the English versions reveal weaknesses that are cultural as much as linguistic (e.g. in *joual*, *le sacre*, the use of English expressions, puns, the conservative rendering of sexual expressions, and inaccurate translations); refers primarily to *La Duchesse de Langeais* and *Hosanna*.

187. Van Toorn, Peter, ed. See 178.

188.   Brassard, André. "Discovering the Nuances." With Renate Usmiani. *Canadian Theatre Review* 24 (Fall 1979): 38-41.

Brassard has directed Tremblay's plays in both French and English and comments on the difficulties with the translated versions of the plays, although the strong characters created by Tremblay "survive the translation"; outlines the problems that arise when staging the play in English.

189.   Claxton, Patricia. "Conversation avec Patricia Claxton, présidente de l'Association des traducteurs littéraires, avec Pierre Marchand." *Histoire de la traduction au Canada*. Numéro spécial de *Meta* 2.1 (mars 1977): 79-87.

Aborde les aspects pratiques de la traduction et du marché littéraire, ainsi que le rôle de l'Association des traducteurs littéraires dans le développement de ce genre de traduction au Canada.

190.   Darras, Jacques. "Traduire Malcolm Lowry, *Under the Volcano*: Entretien avec Jacques Darras." Avec Pierre Mayol. *Esprit* 12 (décembre 1984): 21-27.

Entretien avec Jacques Darras portant sur les difficultés et l'orientation de sa nouvelle traduction de *Under the Volcano* de Malcolm Lowry, sa compréhension de la structure et de l'essence du roman, ainsi que sur certaines fautes d'emphase commises dans la première traduction (*Au-dessous du volcan*, trad. Stephen Spriel et Clarisse Francillon. Paris: Buchet-Chastel, 1963).

191.   Fischman, Sheila. "Sheila Fischman: une schizophrénie très confortable." Avec Jacques Larue-Langlois. *Le Devoir* (24 juillet 1982): 11, 20.

Fischman parle de la façon dont elle est devenue traductrice, de sa technique, de sa relation avec les deux cultures et du livre de Roch Carrier, *La Guerre, Yes Sir!*.

192.   Jones, D.G. "Une ou des littératures canadiennes? Une entrevue avec D.G. Jones." Avec Richard Giguère. *Voix et images* 10.1 (automne 1984): 5-22.

Jones explique pourquoi il traduit de la poésie québécoise, rappelle aussi le rôle qu'a joué F.R. Scott comme traducteur.

193.   Tremblay, Michel. "Where to Begin the Accusation?" With Renate Usmiani. *Canadian Theatre Review* 24 (Fall 1979): 26-37.

Tremblay refers favourably to the different English productions he has seen of *Bonjour, là, bonjour*, and comments on the inevitable loss of flavour in translation, particularly "the folkloric aspect of language."

194.   Van Burek, John. "Tremblay in Translation." With Don Rubin. *Canadian Theatre Review* 24 (Fall 1979): 42-46.

Discusses his practice in translating Tremblay's plays, his and Bill Glassco's problems and choices; comments on the difficulty of rendering Tremblay's vibrant language, particularly *joual*; discusses the translation of specific plays and the difference between translation and adaptation, referring to *Forever Yours, Marie-Lou, Bonjour, là, bonjour*, and *Damnée Manon, sacrée Sandra*; appraises the quality of the translations in collaboration with Glassco, claiming that *Hosanna* and *Les Belles Sœurs* could use further work, and summarizes the general criticisms of *Sainte-Carmen of the Main*; mentions director André Brassard's approach and his responses to the translations.

195. Abley, Mark. Translator's Note. "A Lighted Match: Seven Poems Translated from the French of Émile Nelligan by Mark Abley." *Northern Light* 9 (Spring/Summer 1983): 38-39.

   Discusses his method of translating, referring to instances where he does not remain "faithful . . . to the letter of the French" because he has "tried to be faithful to the tone of the original above all else."

196. Atwood, Margaret. Introduction. *St. Lawrence Blues*. By Marie-Claire Blais. Trans. Ralph Manheim. New York: Bantam, 1976. vii-xvi.

   Comments on the untranslatability of the original title, *Un Joualonais, sa joualonie*, and claims that this difficulty "underlines not only the courage of the translator but the nature of the special situation the book deals with."

197. Barbeau, Marius. Annotations/Commentaires. *Roundelays/Dansons à la ronde*. Danses et jeux populaires recueillis au Canada et en Nouvelle-Angleterre et préparés par Marius Barbeau/Folk dances and games collected in Canada and New England and prepared by Marius Barbeau. Interprétés en anglais par Joy Tranter/Interpreted in English by Joy Tranter. Ottawa: Imprimeur de la Reine et Contrôleur de la Papeterie/Queen's Printer and Controller of Stationery, 1963. 96-97.

   Remarks on Tranter's English adaptations, which "would not submit to the restrictions of mere translation."

   Remarques sur l'adaptation anglaise de Joy Tranter qui ne s'est pas limitée à faire de la traduction littérale.

198. Bergeron, Léandre. Introduction. *The Québécois Dictionary*. Trans. and adapted by Léandre Bergeron. Toronto: James Lorimer and Company, 1982. v-xi.

   Comments on the use and adaptation of English words and expressions in Québécois French; explains that the purpose of the dictionary is to provide contact with Québécois culture for anglophones.

199. Binsse, Harry Lorin. Preface. *In Quest of Splendour*. By Roger Lemelin. Trans. Harry Lorin Binsse. Toronto: McClelland and Stewart, 1955. 7-10.

Outlines the difficulty of translation because of the differences
between French and English educational systems; mentions the
contrast between international French and Lemelin's French.

200. Blake, W.H. Introduction. *Maria Chapdelaine*. By Louis Hémon.
Trans. W.H. Blake. Illus. Thoreau MacDonald. Toronto: Macmillan, 1969. v-xiii.

Focusses on Hémon's use of idiom but comments that "in every
translation lies a double task: easy as it is to turn a book out of
French; to clothe the living spirit in the garment of another language
is difficult indeed."

201. Bonenfant, Joseph. Avant-propos. *Ellipse* 21 (1977): 5-7.

Étudie les différentes théories sur la traduction, le rôle important
qu'elle joue au Canada, pour que les deux cultures apprennent à
se connaître, et au niveau international pour faire connaître les
littératures canadienne-anglaise et québécoise; la signification
culturelle d'*Ellipse* en tant que revue de traduction.

202. Bouraoui, Hédi. Foreword. *Echosmos*. By Hédi Bouraoui. A Bilingual Collection. Oakville, Ontario: Canadian Society for the
Comparative Study of Civilizations and Mosaic Press, 1986. 11.

States that his English versions are not translations but re-creations,
explaining that Keith Harrison's translations "started sounding like
Harrison himself"; in contrast, these are independent creations.

203. Brown, Alan. Translator's Foreword. *Hail Galarneau!*. By Jacques
Godbout. Trans. Alan Brown. Don Mills, Ontario: Longman
Canada, 1970. np.

Claims that the "translator of a novel like *Galarneau* has a strong
and sometimes intimidating feeling of responsibility, for he must
try to be an accurate guide to the slice of French Canada in front
of him"; explicates the difficulty of translating swear words and
slang, gives numerous examples of words and terms not easily
translatable.

204. Browne, Colin. Introductory Notes. *Ellipse 8x8* 29/30 (1982): 6-18.

Discusses the difficulty, the processes, and theories of translation,
and the task of the translator; explains the method of the translation
experiment here, in which the poems were first translated from
their original language and then translated back into their mother

tongue; this process was repeated eight times and involved the participation of eight poets from across Canada.

205. Bruce, Vida. Translator's Note. *Jean Rivard*. By Antoine Gérin-Lajoie. Trans. and with an introduction by Vida Bruce. Toronto: McClelland and Stewart, 1977. 14-15.

Discusses edition used and the omission of certain passages.

206. Chicoine, René. Avertissement. *Rue Saint-Urbain*. Par Mordecai Richler. Trad. René Chicoine. Montréal: Éditions HMH, 1969. 7.

Explique pourquoi les Juifs du roman s'expriment dans la traduction comme des Canadiens français.

207. Claxton, Patricia. Translator's Foreword. *French Kiss Or: A Pang's Progress*. By Nicole Brossard. Trans. Patricia Claxton. Toronto: Coach House Press, 1986. 5-8.

Explains how she has deliberately made her translation more accessible than the original; discusses the authenticity of the translation of historical quotations, the use of markers and aids to indicate English words, allusions to French and Québécois literature and history, the editions used, and her translation practice.

208. Cogswell, Fred. "Émile Nelligan." *The Complete Poems of Émile Nelligan*. Trans. and with an introduction by Fred Cogswell. Montreal: Harvest House, 1983. xvii-xxiv.

Comments on his rendering of Nelligan's poetry into "equivalent" English verse.

209. Cogswell, Fred. Introduction. *The Poetry of Modern Quebec: An Anthology*. Ed. and trans. Fred Cogswell. Montreal: Harvest House, 1976. 5-8.

Comments on the difficulty of translation, the "strange blind spot" encountered when he is unable to find just the right word, and on assistance rendered by others.

210. Colombo, John Robert. Preface. *How Do I Love Thee: Sixty Poets of Canada (and Quebec) select and introduce their favourite poems from their own work*. Ed. John Robert Colombo. Edmonton: M.G. Hurtig, 1970. ix-xv.

Comments on the process of compiling the translations in the anthology and the approaches taken; for example, the French poets checked and revised the translations of their work.

211. Dennis, Gerry, and Alison Hewitt, Donna Murray, and Martha O'Brien. Translator's Note. *The Euguélionne: A Triptych Novel.* By Louky Bersianik. Trans. Gerry Dennis, Alison Hewitt, Donna Murray, and Martha O'Brien. Erin, Ontario: Press Porcépic, 1980. 347.

   Describes the effort to preserve linguistic and stylistic innovations.

212. Dickson, Robert. "En guise d'introduction." *L'Homme invisible/The Invisible Man: un récit/A Story.* Par/By Patrice Desbiens. Sudbury, Ontario: Éditions Prise de Parole/Moonbeam, Ontario: Penumbra Press, 1981. np.

   "Ici, la relation poète-traducteur est assumée par un seul auteur, Patrice Desbiens; le terme 'bilingue de naissance' prend alors de nouvelles dimensions."

213. Downes, Gwladys V. Preface. *when we lie together: Poems from Quebec and Poems by G.V. Downes.* By G.V. Downes. Vancouver: Klanak Press, 1973. 9-11.

   Enumerates problems of translating French poems into English, the high standards set by F.R. Scott, and outlines three styles of translation: extremely free, literal fidelity, occasional departures from literal accuracy.

214. Ellenwood, [William] Ray. Introduction and Translator's Note. *Entrails.* By Claude Gauvreau. Trans. Ray Ellenwood. Toronto: Coach House Press, 1981. 7-18.

   Outlines problems caused by Gauvreau's style, his approach and method as the translator, and possible flaws in his translation.

215. Ellenwood, [William] Ray. Translator's Note. *Quince Jam.* By Jacques Ferron. Trans. Ray Ellenwood. Toronto: Coach House Press, 1977. 9-12.

   Identifies text on which translation is based.

216. Ellenwood, [William] Ray. "Welcome to Broke City." *Broke City.* By Jacques Renaud. Trans. David Homel. Montreal: Guernica Editions, 1984. 7-11.

   Discusses the scarcity of literary translation in Canada; criticizes the first translation of Renaud's novel and concludes with a summary of what makes Homel's translation good: because "the whole question of *joual* is underplayed," the novel does not read like a translation or seem irrelevant to the anglophone reader.

217. Ellis, David. Note. *Dragon Island*. By Jacques Godbout. Trans. David Ellis. Don Mills, Ontario: Musson, 1978. np.

    Remarks on the incorporation of "a number of minor alterations of the original text" in the translation, and accepts responsibility for any errors that occur.

218. Fischman, Sheila. Translator's Foreword. *Is It the Sun, Philibert?* By Roch Carrier. Trans. Sheila Fischman. Toronto: Anansi, 1972. 1-3.

    Discusses the translation of colloquial language, particularly swear words.

219. Fischman, Sheila. Translator's Note. *Jack Kerouac: a chicken essay*. By Victor-Lévy Beaulieu. Trans. Sheila Fischman. Toronto: Coach House Press, 1975. np.

    Comments on the use of *joual* and her decision to leave parts of the text in French.

220. Fischman, Sheila. Translator's Note. *La Guerre, Yes Sir!*. By Roch Carrier. Trans. Sheila Fischman. Toronto: Anansi, 1970. 1-3.

    Outlines her approach to colloquial language and swear words; includes a brief glossary of some of the French terms used in the text.

221. Frye, Northrop. Foreword/Préface. Trad. Jean Simard. *Dialogue sur la traduction à propos du Tombeau des rois*. Par Anne Hébert et Frank Scott. Montréal: Éditions HMH, 1970. 11-21.

    Argues that poetry can be translated, contrary to Robert Frost's assertion that the essence of poetry is lost in translation; discusses the communication of a poem's meaning through translation, particularly as this relates to the difference between translation that is literal and translation that is "faithful only to the general spirit of the original."

    Affirme que la poésie peut être traduite, contrairement à l'argument de Robert Frost selon lequel l'essence de la poésie est perdue dans la traduction; parle de la manière dont la signification d'un poème est communiquée au moyen de la traduction, illustrant notamment dans ce cas la différence qui existe entre une traduction littérale et une traduction "uniquement fidèle à l'esprit général de l'original."

222.   Gagnon, François-Marc and Dennis Young. Notes des traducteurs/
        Translators' Note. *Écrits/Writings 1942-1958*. By Paul-Émile Bor-
        duas. Présentés et édités par/Introduced and edited by François-
        Marc Gagnon. Trad./trans. François-Marc Gagnon and Dennis
        Young. Halifax: The Nova Scotia College of Art and Design,
        1978. 7-9.

        Cette "note" traite du style de Borduas et de la nécessité d'apporter
        quelques changements et une certaine clarification au procédé de
        traduction.

        "Note" discusses Borduas's style and the necessity for some
        changes and clarification in the process of translation.

223.   Gaulin, Michel. "A Note on the Text." *The Iron Wedge/L'Appel de
        la race*. By Lionel Groulx. Trans. J.S. Wood. Ed. and intro. by
        Michel Gaulin. Ottawa: Carleton University Press, 1986. xxxii-
        xxxiii.

        Outlines the edition used and rationale for the translation of the
        title.

224.   Gertler, Maynard. Editor's Note. *The Impertinences of Brother
        Anonymous*. Trans. Miriam Chapin. Montreal: Harvest House,
        1962 (1965). 9-11.

        Reflects briefly on the translatability of the book (a rebuttal to
        those who would claim it is "untranslatable").

225.   Glassco, John. Introduction. "To Sir John A. MacDonald." By
        Louis Riel. Trans. John Glassco. *Canadian Literature* 37 (Summer
        1968): 40.

        Comments on the necessary liberties he took to provide a faithful,
        if not entirely literal translation of Riel's poem.

226.   Glassco, John. Introduction. *The Complete Poems of Saint-Denys
        Garneau*. Trans. and with an introduction by John Glassco. Ottawa:
        Oberon Press, 1975. 5-17.

        Asserts the importance and possibility of successfully translating
        poetry; describes his method of translating Garneau: the "render-
        ings are faithful but not literal."

227.   Glassco, John. Introduction. *The Poetry of French Canada in
        Translation*. Ed. John Glassco. Toronto: Oxford University Press,
        1970. xvii-xxiv.

Remarks on the history and practice of translation, drawn from "The Opaque Medium" [see 48].

228. Godard, Barbara. "Flying Away with Language." *Lesbian Triptych.* By Jovette Marchessault. Trans. Yvonne Klein. Toronto: Women's Press, 1985. 9-28.

Suggests that when "transcoding a set of meanings from one language into another, it sometimes happens that things are radically revised . . . meaning may be lost" and sometimes "meaning is gained"; gives examples of both instances in Klein's "fine translation."

229. Godard, Barbara. Preface. *Lovhers.* By Nicole Brossard. Trans. Barbara Godard. Montreal: Guernica Editions, 1986. 7-12.

Comments on the two contradictory roles of prefaces in translated texts; speculates on the relationship between a history of theories of translation and a history of the preface as a genre; describes the "special problems posed in translating this work from French into English," such as the "doubleness and multiplicity of meaning created through puns, ellipses, and portmanteau words"; discusses the history of this translation and the translator as ventriloquist [see 55].

230. Godard, Barbara. Preface. *These Our Mothers Or: The Disintegrating Chapter.* By Nicole Brossard. Trans. Barbara Godard. Toronto: Coach House Press, 1983. np.

Explains how she transmits Brossard's language play.

231. Godbout, Jacques. Introduction. *La Grande Muraille de Chine.* Par John Robert Colombo. Trad. Jacques Godbout. Montréal: Éditions du Jour, 1968. np.

Rapide description de la traduction des noms chinois en français.

232. Hay, Peter. Introduction. *The Trial of Jean-Baptiste M.* By Robert Gurik. Trans. Allan Van Meer. Vancouver: Talonbooks, 1974. 5-8.

Discusses the role of translation in the lack of English-Canadian access to Québécois theatre.

233. Heller, Zelda. Afterword. *Aux yeux des hommes.* Par John Herbert. Trad. René Dionne. Montréal: Leméac, 1971. 101-103. Rpt. from *The Montreal Star* 20 April 1970.

Comments on the success of this translation: how Dionne has "recreated the text," capturing the spirit of the original.

234. Hewitt, Alison. See 211.

235. Jones, D.G. Introduction. *The Terror of the Snows*. By Paul-Marie Lapointe. Trans. D.G. Jones. Pittsburgh: University of Pittsburgh Press, 1976. xi-xv.

 More a discussion of Lapointe's poems than of Jones's translation, yet reveals an implicit explication of Jones's mode of translation.

236. La Bossière, Camille R. Introduction. *Translation in Canadian Literature: Symposium 1982*. Reappraisals: Canadian Writers 9. Ed. and with an introduction by Camille R. La Bossière. Ottawa: University of Ottawa Press, 1983. 9-12.

 Brief summary of articles at the 1982 symposium in Ottawa; suggests that the process is more interesting than the product of translation and should be studied further.

237. Lasnier, Rina. Avant-dire. "Poems by A.J.M. Smith." Trans. Rina Lasnier. *Canadian Literature* 39 (Winter 1969): 27-28.

 Description poétique de l'expérience qu'elle a vécue en traduisant de la poésie: "transposer . . . est l'expression juste."

238. Lebel, Maurice. Avant-propos. *Histoire littéraire du Canada*. Édit. Carl F. Klinck. Trad. Maurice Lebel. Québec: Les Presses de l'Université Laval, 1970. 7-8.

 Rapide commentaire portant sur son approche pour traduire des citations et l'index.

239. Lobdell, David. Translator's Note. *Letter by Letter*. By Louise Maheux-Forcier. Trans. David Lobdell. Ottawa: Oberon Press, 1982. np.

 Explains how and why titles and the order of stories were changed in translation, and why "La Queue," which relies almost exclusively for its effect upon a play of words that cannot be translated, was omitted.

240. Marcotte, Gilles. Introduction. *The Journal of Saint-Denys Garneau*. Trans. John Glassco. Introduction by Gilles Marcotte. Toronto: McClelland and Stewart, 1962. 9-15.

 Includes a discussion of the difficulty of translating poetry; comments on the significance of this translation because it is the first of its kind, and because it provides insight into the author and his background—it is important to "the cultural framework in which we are living."

241. Marshall, Joyce. Introduction. *The Road Past Altamont*. By Gabrielle Roy. Trans. Joyce Marshall. Toronto: McClelland and Stewart, 1966. vii-xi.

Comments on the translator's role, particularly as s/he develops "a knowledge of the structure and intricacy of the book that few ordinary readers could have," and thereby is more likely to be aware of flaws in the original work; also a discussion of Roy's close involvement with the translation of her writing, her exacting "ear" for language, and the result that the translation is "as close to the original vision as two brains can get it."

242. Marshall, Joyce. Introduction. *Word from New France: The Selected Letters of Marie de l'Incarnation*. Trans. and ed. Joyce Marshall. Toronto: Oxford University Press, 1967. 1-33.

Discusses a few of her particular decisions regarding methodology.

243. McGee, Robert. Translator's Note. *Small Horses and Intimate Beasts*. By Michel Garneau. Trans. Robert McGee. Montreal: Véhicule Press, 1985. 15.

Comments that "equivalent music in the English of my own voice is what I have sought to render," and that he is "grateful for Michel's inside information."

244. McPherson, Hugo. Introduction. *The Tin Flute*. By Gabrielle Roy. Trans. Hannah Josephson. Toronto: McClelland and Stewart, 1969. v-xi.

Comments on the inability of the translation to capture the French-Canadian accent, idiom, and profanities of the original, and claims that "very often the French comes through beautifully by undergoing a sea-change," as in the title.

245. Melançon, Robert. Préface. *Blind Painting*. By Robert Melançon. Trans. Philip Stratford. Montreal: Signal Editions, 1985. 11.

Explique comment la traduction de ces poèmes lui a donné envie de les réviser; un poète "n'est jamais qu'un traducteur qui transpose en mots, le moins mal possible, ce qui, peut-être, échappe aux mots" [voir 270].

246. Murray, Donna. See 211.

247. Nadeau, Maurice. Introduction. *Lunar caustic*. Par Malcolm Lowry. Trad. Clarisse Francillon. Traduction revue; *Le Caustique lunaire*. Par Malcolm Lowry. Trad. Michèle d'Astorg et Clarisse Francillon. Version définitive de Clarisse Francillon. Paris: Les Lettres nouvelles/Maurice Nadeau, 1977. np.

Retrace l'histoire des différents manuscrits et versions de ce texte et de ses traductions.

248. O'Brien, Martha. See 211.

249. O'Connor, John. Introduction. *Fear's Folly (Les Demi-civilisés)*. By Jean-Charles Harvey. Trans. John Glassco. Ottawa: Carleton University Press, 1982. 1-24.

Discusses details of Glassco's translation as well as an earlier translation, *Sackcloth for Banner*, by Jean-Charles Harvey, trans. Lukin Barette; judges the latter poor in comparison with Glassco's articulate translation.

250. Pentland, Jane. Introduction. "All the Way Home." By Gabrielle Poulin. Trans. Jane Pentland. *Matrix* 15 (Spring/Summer 1982): 18-20.

Discusses her translation of two chapters of Gabrielle Poulin's *Cogne la caboche* and the specific problems encountered: the title; tense; flow from dream to narrative to monologue; Canadian idioms; metaphor and dual meanings.

251. Peraldi, François. "Afterword: The Last Cartographers." *The Passions of Mister Desire (Selected Poems)*. By André Roy. Trans. Daniel Sloate. Montreal: Guernica Editions, 1986. 75-81.

Describes in a theoretical context his ideas on how the "real work involved in poetic translation is on the level of the speaker-poet's signifier chain," and gives examples from Sloate's translation.

252. Plourde, Marc. "On Translating Miron: A Commentary." *Embers and Earth (Selected Poems)*. By Gaston Miron. Trans. D.G. Jones and Marc Plourde. With an introduction by D.G. Jones and a Translator's Commentary by Marc Plourde. Bilingual Edition. Montreal: Guernica Editions, 1984. 113-122. Rpt. in *The Insecurity of Art: Essays on Poetics*. Ed. Ken Norris and Peter Van Toorn. Montreal: Véhicule Press, 1982. 108-114.

Discusses the difficulties of translating and his own method; outlines the problems and choices faced when translating Miron.

253. Putnam, Samuel. Introductory Note. *The Town Below*. By Roger Lemelin. Trans. Samuel Putnam. Toronto: McClelland and Stewart, 1961. v-xii.

Explains the meaning of a few untranslatable terms that are used to describe characters in the novel; comments on the difficulty of translating the "peculiarities" of the French and the "frequent psychological subtleties of the narrative."

254. Robinson, Michelle. Note de la traductrice. *Louis Riel: la fin d'un rêve*. Par Rudy Wiebe. Trad. Michelle Robinson. Montréal: Éditions Pierre Tisseyre, 1985. np.

"Note de la traductrice" explique son utilisation du terme "Sauvages" pour rendre "Indians" dans la traduction qu'elle a faite de *The Scorched-Wood People* de Wiebe.

255. Roy, G.R. Introduction. *Douze poètes modernes du Canada français/ Twelve Modern French Canadian Poets*. Trad./Trans. G.R. Roy. Texte français/with French Text. Toronto: Éditions Ryerson/The Ryerson Press, 1948. v-vi.

Comments on the importance of translating modern French-Canadian texts for the English reader; the cultural need for translations; defends the necessity for literary translation.

256. Sabiston, Elizabeth. Introduction. *Echosmos*. By Hédi Bouraoui. A Bilingual Collection. Oakville, Ontario: Canadian Society for the Comparative Study of Civilizations and Mosaic Press, 1986. np.

Describes how the poet "has prepared himself, not English translations, but English versions of his French poetry for this bilingual edition," and bridges the two languages to create "bonds between and among the 'three solitudes' of Canada: the Anglophone, Francophone . . . and the multicultural groups."

257. Sanderson, Gertrude. Preface. *Within the Mystery*. By Jacques Brault. Trans. Gertrude Sanderson. Montreal: Guernica Editions, 1986. 7-8.

Comments on how she began translating these poems.

258. Scott, F.R. Preface. *Poems of French Canada*. Trans. F.R. Scott. Burnaby, B.C.: Blackfish Press, 1975. i-vi. Rpt. in *The Insecurity*

of Art: Essays on Poetics. Ed. Ken Norris and Peter Van Toorn. Montreal: Véhicule Press, 1982. 115-120.

Discusses his interest in and personal acquaintance with Quebec poets, including Saint-Denys Garneau, Anne Hébert, and Gaston Miron, his desire to translate their work, his own background in French and French-Canadian literature, and the literary scene in Quebec in the 40s and 50s.

259.   Scott, F.R. Translator's Note. *St.-Denys Garneau and Anne Hébert*. Trans. F.R. Scott. Vancouver: Klanak Press, 1962. 9.

Outlines reasons for translating the two poets and his philosophy on translation: "a prejudice for literalness."

260.   Shouldice, Larry. Preface. *Contemporary Quebec Criticism*. Ed. and trans. Larry Shouldice. Toronto: University of Toronto Press, 1979. vii-ix.

Describes practice of "providing an acceptable English version of the essays while maintaining as much as possible of the style and character of the original French."

261.   Shouldice, Larry. Foreword. *Ellipse* 17 (1975): 6-7.

Responds to Fraser Sutherland's criticism that the translations in *Ellipse* were "too cautious and timid," and comments on difficulties of translating concrete poetry.

262.   Shouldice, Larry. Foreword. *Ellipse* 20 (1977): 9-11.

Asserts that translation is "always at least an implied act of comparison" as he explains the juxtaposition and comparison of Jean-Aubert Loranger and W.W.E. Ross.

263.   Shouldice, Larry. Foreword. *Ellipse* 27/28 (1981): 6-7.

Reflects on translation as comparison and *Ellipse*'s function as a journal of translation; states that both Al Purdy's "compacted, elliptical syntax" and Michel Garneau's "deceptive simplicity and directness . . . are difficult to translate, and for very different reasons."

264.   Simard, Jean. Introduction. *Mon père, ce héros* . . . . Par Mordecai Richler. Trad. Jean Simard. Montréal: Le Cercle du Livre de France, 1975. 11-12.

Explique pourquoi il a traduit le roman de Richler.

265. Sloate, Daniel. Preface. *First Secrets and Other Poems*. By Éloi de Grandmont. Trans. Daniel Sloate. Bilingual Edition. Montreal: Guernica Editions, 1983. 7-8.

   "I have tried to convey as faithfully as possible . . . the phonetic texture in the poems and the rhythms."

266. Sloate, Daniel. Translator's Comments. *The Passions of Mister Desire (Selected Poems)*. By André Roy. Trans. Daniel Sloate. Montreal: Guernica Editions, 1986. 7-10.

   Explains the difficulty of this translation and how he tried to "transpose" the "syntax-shattering," the "phonic texture," "stammering," "ellipses," and "poetic ethos."

267. Sterling, Sharon. Editor's Note. *A Poetry of Frontiers: Comparative Studies in Quebec/Canadian Literature*. By Clément Moisan. Trans. George Lang and Linda Weber. Victoria/Toronto: Press Porcépic, 1983. np.

   Discusses the process of this translation—the consultations between the author and translator and the "extensive editing and revision," with the result that this "is a work which we feel is a clear expression of Clément Moisan's ideas and a valuable contribution to the field of comparative literature."

268. Stevens, John. Introduction. *Modern Canadian Stories*. Ed. John Stevens. New York: Bantam Books, 1975. ix-xv.

   Refers not to the quality of the three stories in translation, but to the scarcity of available translation, the recent increase in translation, and the potential unity of the two solitudes in Canadian culture.

269. Stratford, Philip. Foreword/Préface. *Bibliography of Canadian Books in Translation: French to English and English to French/Bibliographie de livres canadiens traduits de l'anglais au français et du français à l'anglais*. See/voir 131.

270. Stratford, Philip. Translator's Note. *Blind Painting*. By Robert Melançon. Trans. Philip Stratford. Montreal: Signal Editions, 1985. 10.

   Comments on the relationship between translator and poet, and their relationship with the translated poems: "these poems . . . continued to change on both sides of the centre crease" [see 245].

271. Stratford, Philip. Translator's Preface. *Convergence: Essays from Quebec*. By Jean Le Moyne. Trans. Philip Stratford. Toronto: The Ryerson Press, 1966. ix-xii.

    Comments on Le Moyne's style and how he has tried to retain it; also mentions some changes, and omissions which would be of less interest to an English public.

272. Sutherland, Ronald. Introduction. *Dust Over the City*. By André Langevin. Trans. John Latrobe and Robert Gottlieb. Toronto: McClelland and Stewart, 1955. Rpt. Toronto: NCL, 1974. np.

    Includes a brief comment about the inability of translation to capture all the "niceties of an author's style," but none the less Langevin's "sensitive use of imagery" is communicated in this translation.

273. Thomas, Clara. Introduction. *Canadians of Old*. By Philippe-Joseph Aubert de Gaspé. Trans. Charles G.D. Roberts. Introduction by Clara Thomas. Toronto: McClelland and Stewart, 1974. 7-12.

    Gives a history of the translations of the text and shows how Roberts's version is literal.

274. Tisseyre, Michelle. "Jean Simard." *Mon père, ce héros* . . . Par Mordecai Richler. Trad. Jean Simard. Montréal: Le Cercle du Livre de France, 1975. np.

    Note sur Jean Simard, traducteur.

275. Williams, Penny. Translator's Note. *Knife on the Table*. By Jacques Godbout. Trans. Penny Williams. Toronto: McClelland and Stewart, 1968. xv.

    Explains that the English in the source text is indicated by italics in the target text.

276. Young, Dennis. Voir/see 222.

277. Audet, Noël. "*Poèmes des quatre côtés.*" Compte rendu des *Poèmes des quatre côtés*, de Jacques Brault. Saint-Lambert: Éditions du Noroît, 1975. *Voix et images* 1.1 (septembre 1975): 131-134.

Examine en détail la théorie de Brault sur la nontraduction et sa mise en pratique et donne des exemples de nontraduction; Audet signale l'impossibilité de traduire de la poésie et la trahison de la traduction littéraire; il suggère que la nontraduction n'est pas un terme approprié, qu'elle "ne fait qu'indiquer la volonté du poète de s'éloigner d'une traduction littérale, sans marquer les aspects positifs de sa démarche" [voir 174].

278. Beaver, John. "A Selection of Quebec Contemporary Fiction." Rev. of *Fanny*, by Louis Dantin, trans. Ray Chamberlain. Montreal: Harvest House, 1973; *The Saint-Elias*, by Jacques Ferron, trans. Pierre Cloutier. Montreal: Harvest House, 1975; and *The Juneberry Tree*, by Jacques Ferron, trans. Ray Chamberlain. Montreal: Harvest House, 1975. *Quill & Quire* 41.10 (October 1975): 17.

Discusses publication of translations by Harvest House in the French Writers of Canada series—the purpose of the publishers is to make French "literary and social trends" available in English Canada; mentions the recurring critique of translation which claims that translation can never convey the complete intent and tone of the original. Questions the value of translating an insignificant novel like *Fanny*; comments on the skill of the translations of Ferron's books, considering his unique style.

279. Cavell, Richard A. "Transliterature." Rev. of *Translation in Canadian Literature*, ed. Camille R. La Bossière. Ottawa: University of Ottawa Press, 1983; *Driving Home: A Dialogue Between Writers and Readers*, eds. Barbara Belyea and Estelle Dansereau. Waterloo, Ontario: Wilfrid Laurier University Press for the Calgary Institute for the Humanities, 1984; and *The Man With a Flower in His Mouth*, by Gilles Archambault, trans. David Lobdell. Ottawa: Oberon Press, 1983. *Canadian Literature* 106 (Fall 1985): 108-110.

Includes a historical overview of translation in Canada; review is concerned with a summary of the ideas expressed in the two books of essays; focusses on *Translation in Canadian Literature*, with particular reference to Philip Stratford and his article on the translation of Antonine Maillet's novel *Pélagie* [see 128], and to essays by E.D. Blodgett, Ray Ellenwood, Richard Giguère, and

Larry Shouldice [see 8; 34; 46; 121]; concludes with a brief analysis of how the Archambault book "grounds a number of these critical aperçus."

280.   Claxton, Patricia D. "Culture Vulture." Rev. of *Prochain épisode*, by Hubert Aquin, trans. Penny Williams. Toronto: McClelland and Stewart, 1967. *Meta* 12.1 (mars 1967): 9-13.

First gives examples of translation errors in *Prochain épisode* and *The Tin Flute*, and then points out the need for good translations and translators; urges establishment of training programmes, an annual prize, and a vigilant committee.

281.   Davies, Gillian. "Of Princes and Scarecrows: A Look at Contemporary Quebec Fiction." Rev. of *The Princes*, by Jacques Benoît, trans. David Lobdell. Ottawa: Oberon Press, 1977; *Children of the Black Sabbath*, by Anne Hébert, trans. Carol Dunlop-Hébert. Don Mills, Ontario: Musson, 1977; and *The Scarecrows of Saint-Emmanuel*, by André Major, trans. Sheila Fischman. Toronto: McClelland and Stewart, 1977. *Queen's Quarterly* 85.3 (Autumn 1978): 447-452.

Brief comments on the three translators Sheila Fischman, David Lobdell, and Carol Dunlop-Hébert, and on Fischman's "dexterous handling" of *joual* and of Major's title *L'Épouvantail*.

282.   Davis, Frances. Rev. of *Orphan Street*, by André Langevin, trans. Alan Brown. Toronto: McClelland and Stewart, 1976. *Dalhousie Review* 57.1 (Spring 1977): 162-165.

Includes a discussion of translation in general and an overview of possible approaches; questions whether or not it is sufficient for translation to do no more than "faithfully" render the plot of the novel into English prose and criticizes Brown's translation as having failed to show "empathy with the material." Gives examples of the inadequate rendering of slang and of too literal translations.

283.   Ferres, John H. "Poetics and Polemics." Rev. of *The Insecurity of Art: Essays on Poetics*, eds. Ken Norris and Peter Van Toorn. Montreal: Véhicule Press, 1982. *Essays on Canadian Writing* 30 (Winter 1984-1985): 153-159.

Comments on the "vexing question of translation" in the "overview of poetic politics of Quebec"; outlines the concerns and activities of translators Frank Scott and D.G. Jones.

284. Garebian, Keith. "Liberation in the Rag-and-Bone Shop." Rev. of *Les Belles Sœurs* and *Hosanna*, by Michel Tremblay, trans. John Van Burek and Bill Glassco. Vancouver: Talonbooks, 1974. *Canadian Literature* 66 (Autumn 1975): 112-116.

Discusses the difficulty of translating *joual* and the resulting loss of "the linguistic rhythm and cadences of the original" in *Les Belles Sœurs*; contrasts *Hosanna*, which is a more successful translation because *joual* is less significant.

285. Herlan, James. "Quebec Criticism in Translation: The Ideology of Aesthetics." Rev. of *Contemporary Quebec Criticism*, ed. and trans. Larry Shouldice. Toronto: University of Toronto Press, 1979. *Essays on Canadian Writing* 26 (Summer 1983): 150-168.

Comments on Shouldice's skill as translator, the smoothness of the translations, the significance of the translation of this anthology in facilitating comparison of the two literatures, and on translator as comparatist.

286. Kröller, Eva-Marie. "Shadows of the Past." Rev. of *In the Shadow of the Wind*, by Anne Hébert, trans. Sheila Fischman. Toronto: Stoddart, 1983. *Canadian Literature* 103 (Winter 1984): 129-131.

Analyzes the translation at length; compares the translation with the original; outlines two instances where "Fischman had unduly departed from the original"; discusses the "patterns and effects in Hébert's prose that are lost in translation."

287. Macri, Francis M. "Not Simply a Problem of CahinCaha." Rev. of *The Torrent*, by Anne Hébert, trans. Gwendolyn Moore. Montreal: Harvest House, 1973. *Laurentian University Review/Revue de l'Université Laurentienne* 7.1 (November 1974): 86-93.

Detailed comparison of original and translation; focusses on the unstylistic English and frequent mistranslations.

288. Merler, Grazia. "Translation and the Creation of Cultural Myths in Canada." Rev. of *The Silent Rooms*, by Anne Hébert, trans. Kathy Mezei. Don Mills, Ontario: Musson, 1974; and *The Complete Poems of Saint-Denys Garneau*, trans. John Glassco. Ottawa: Oberon Press, 1975. *West Coast Review* 11.2 (October 1976): 26-33.

Begins with a substantial discussion of the role and art of translation; comments on the general anonymity of the translator and the development and increase of translation in Canada. Summarizes Glassco's views on translation as stated in his introduction [see 226], and compares the literary approaches of Hébert and Garneau; suggests that these translations demonstrate "how translation can be a powerful tool in either the creation or the perpetuation of cultural myths"; analyzes and contrasts the two translations.

289. Mezei, Kathy. "Letters in Canada 1982: Translations." Rev. of *Pélagie: The Return to a Homeland*, by Antonine Maillet, trans. Philip Stratford; *Sweet Madness*, by Robert Lalonde, trans. David Homel; *One for the Road*, by Gilles Archambault, trans. David Lobdell; *The First Person*, by Pierre Turgeon, trans. David Lobdell; *Letter by Letter*, by Louise Maheux-Forcier, trans. David Lobdell; *The Neighbour and Other Stories*, by Naïm Kattan, trans. Judith Madley and Patricia Claxton; *Héloïse*, by Anne Hébert, trans. Sheila Fischman; *The Fragile Lights of Earth*, by Gabrielle Roy, trans. Alan Brown; *The Fairies Are Thirsty*, by Denise Boucher, trans. Alan Brown; *Jos Connaissant*, by Victor-Lévy Beaulieu, trans. Ray Chamberlain; *No Big Deal*, by the Archambault Prison Theatre Group, trans. David Homel; and *Interlude*, by Robert Marteau, trans. Barry Callaghan. *The University of Toronto Quarterly* 52.4 (Summer 1983): 385-397.

Detailed analysis of translations; subjects covered: critics' theories; situation; editorial details; dialect; sexual difference; translation of titles; lexical and stylistic errors; *joual*; dramatic adaptation; gender in translation.

290. Mezei, Kathy. "Letters in Canada 1983: Translations." Rev. of *Ellipse 8X8* 29/30 (1982); *TESSERA* 1, in *Room of One's Own* 8.4 (1983); *The Oxford Book of French-Canadian Short Stories*, ed. Richard Teleky; *Canada's Lost Plays—Colonial Quebec: French-Canadian Drama, 1606-1966*, ed. Anton Wagner; *The Complete Poems of Émile Nelligan*, trans. Fred Cogswell; *The Alchemy of the Body and Other Poems*, by Juan Garcia, trans. Marc Plourde; *Concrete City: Selected Poems 1972-1982*, by Claude Beausoleil, trans. Ray Chamberlain; *First Secrets and Other Poems*, by Éloi de Grandmont, trans. Daniel Sloate; *Fear's Folly (Les demi-civilisés)*, by Jean-Charles Harvey, trans. John Glassco; *Best Man*, by Claire Martin, trans. David Lobdell; *The Man With a Flower in His Mouth*, by Gilles Archambault, trans. David Lobdell; *Sweet Poison/Coming Soon*, by Pierre Turgeon, trans. David Lobdell; *Hooked on Elvis*, by André Major, trans. David Lobdell; *In the*

Shadow of the Wind, by Anne Hébert, trans. Sheila Fischman; *These Our Mothers Or: The Disintegrating Chapter*, by Nicole Brossard, trans. Barbara Godard; and *Saga of the Wet Hens*, by Jovette Marchessault, trans. Linda Gaboriau. *The University of Toronto Quarterly* 53.4 (Summer 1984): 391-410.

Detailed analysis of translations; subjects covered: loss and gain in translation; editorial details; editions; history of translated text; neologisms; word play; English-French relations; critics' theories; practice; situation; sexual difference; dialect; colloquialisms; translation of poetry; stylistic and lexical errors; gender in translation; translation of prose; treatment of English expressions in translating from French source text; equivalence; cultural context.

291. Mezei, Kathy. "Letters in Canada 1984: Translations." Rev. of "The Witch and the Barley Seed" and "The Cup of Tea," two short stories by Jacques Ferron, trans. Wayne Grady; *Alice et Gertrude, Natalie et Renée et ce cher Ernest*, by Jovette Marchessault, trans. Basil Kingstone; and an excerpt from *L'Échappée des discours de l'œil*, by Madeleine Ouellette-Michalska, trans. Sue Stewart in *A Decade of Quebec Fiction*. Special number of *Canadian Fiction Magazine* 47 (1983); "The House on the Esplanade," by Anne Hébert, trans. Morna Scott Stoddart and "Discretion," by Louise Maheux-Forcier, trans. Sally Livingstone in *Stories by Canadian Women*, ed. Rosemary Sullivan; *Surrealism and Quebec Literature: History of a Cultural Revolution*, by André G. Bourassa, trans. Mark Czarnecki; *Contemporary Quebec Criticism*, ed. and trans. Larry Shouldice; *The Death of André Breton*, by Jean Yves Collette, trans. Ray Chamberlain; *Broke City*, by Jacques Renaud, trans. David Homel; *Selected Tales of Jacques Ferron*, trans. Betty Bednarski; *Lady With Chains*, by Roch Carrier, trans. Sheila Fischman; *Thérèse and Pierrette and the Little Hanging Angel*, by Michel Tremblay, trans. Sheila Fischman; *The Crime of Ovide Plouffe*, by Roger Lemelin, trans. Alan Brown; *Moon Country*, by Denys Chabot, trans. David Lobdell; *The Master of Strappado*, by Négovan Rajic, trans. David Lobdell; *All the Way Home*, by Gabrielle Poulin, trans. Jane Pentland; *Veiled Countries/Lives*, by Marie-Claire Blais, trans. Michael Harris; *Embers and Earth (Selected Poems)*, by Gaston Miron, trans. D.G. Jones and Marc Plourde; *Spells of Fury*, by Michel Beaulieu, trans. Arlette Francière; and *Voiceless People*, by Marco Micone, trans. Maurizia Binda. *The University of Toronto Quarterly* 54.4 (Summer 1985): 383-399.

Detailed analysis of translations; subjects covered: sexual difference; translation of feminist discourse; *faux amis*; word play; situation; editorial details; history of translated text; transposition; literal translation; treatment of English expressions in translating from French source text; *joual*; equivalence; cultural context; English-French relations; neologisms; stylistic and lexical errors; loss and gain in translation; translation of titles; cultural myths generated by translation; translation of poetry; free translation; diglossia.

292.   Mezei, Kathy. "Letters in Canada 1985: Translations." Rev. of *Mario*, by Claude Jasmin, trans. David Lobdell; *Anna's World*, by Marie-Claire Blais, trans. Sheila Fischman; *Champagne and Opium*, by Alain Grandbois, trans. Larry Shouldice; *The Penniless Redeemer*, by Jacques Ferron, trans. Ray Ellenwood; *Monsieur Melville*, by Victor-Lévy Beaulieu, trans. Ray Chamberlain; *Mauve*, by Nicole Brossard, trans. Daphne Marlatt; *The Clarity of Voices (Selected Poems: 1974-1981)*, by Philippe Haeck, trans. Antonio d'Alfonso; *fragile moments*, by Jacques Brault, trans. Barry Callaghan; *The Fifth Season*, by Paul-Marie Lapointe, trans. D.G. Jones; *Remember Me*, by Michel Tremblay, trans. John Stowe; and *Lesbian Triptych*, by Jovette Marchessault, trans. Yvonne Klein. *The University of Toronto Quarterly* 56.1 (Fall 1986): 72-82.

Detailed analysis of translations; subjects covered: translation as treason; critics' theories; treatment of English expressions in translating from French source text; translation of titles; cultural context; colloquialisms; history of translated text; linguistic context; word play; literal and faithful translation; loss and gain in translation; transformation; English-French relations; translation of feminist discourse; translation of poetry; neologisms; *faux amis*; sexual difference; gender in translation; act of translation; situation.

293.   Mezei, Kathy. "Like the Wind Made Visible." Rev. of *The Complete Poems of Saint-Denys Garneau*, trans. John Glassco. Ottawa: Oberon Press, 1974. *Canadian Literature* 71 (Winter 1976): 83-87.

Discusses the necessity for and role of translation; praises Glassco's translation as sensitive and claims that the translation often clarifies "some of the elusiveness of Garneau without . . . losing the grace and subtlety of the French."

294.   Mezei, Kathy. "Translations." Rev. of *The Poems of French Canada*,
        trans. F.R. Scott. Burnaby, B.C.: Blackfish Press, 1975. *Canadian
        Literature* 79 (Winter 1978): 103-106.

        Detailed discussion of Scott's role as a translator; some comparison
        of his translations with those of Alan Brown and John Glassco—
        Scott is "more literal . . . yet he invariably demonstrates an
        unerring instinct for the appropriate word or phrase, or the right
        rhythm."

295.   Nepveu, Pierre. Compte rendu d'*Élégies civiles*, par Dennis Lee,
        trad. Marc Lebel. Montréal: Éditions de l'Hexagone, 1980. *Livres
        et auteurs québécois* (1980): 116-117.

        Critique détaillée de la traduction de Lebel qui est "particulière-
        ment inadéquate dans la première moitié du recueil."

296.   O'Connor, John. "Letters in Canada 1976: Translations." Rev. of
        *Bibliography of Canadian Books in Translation: French to English
        and English to French/Bibliographie de livres canadiens traduits
        de l'anglais au français et du français à l'anglais*, by Maureen
        Newman and Philip Stratford; *Canadian Fiction: An Annotated
        Bibliography*, by Margery Fee and Ruth Cawker; *The Madman,
        the Kite and the Island*, by Félix Leclerc, trans. Philip Stratford;
        Enchanted Summer, by Gabrielle Roy, trans. Joyce Marshall;
        Master of the River, by Félix-Antoine Savard, trans. Richard
        Howard; *Marie Calumet*, by Rodolphe Girard, trans. Irène Currie;
        The Brawl, by Gérard Bessette, trans. Marc Lebel and Ronald
        Sutherland; *Orphan Street*, by André Langevin, trans. Alan Brown;
        Dürer's Angel, by Marie-Claire Blais, trans. David Lobdell; *The
        Execution*, by Marie-Claire Blais, trans. David Lobdell; *The Poetry
        of Modern Quebec: An Anthology*, ed. and trans. Fred Cogswell;
        and *Ellipse* 18 and 19. *The University of Toronto Quarterly* 46.4
        (Summer 1977): 399-415.

        Detailed analysis of translations; subjects covered: history of
        literary translation in Canada; situation; translation of titles; capture
        of tone; lexical and stylistic errors; dialect; literal translation;
        editions; editorial details; translation of dialogue; *joual*; presence
        of English expressions in French source text; treatment of English
        expressions in translating from French source text; equivalence;
        retention of French in English translation; English-French relations.

297.   O'Connor, John. "Letters in Canada 1977: Translations." Rev. of
        Ellipse 20 and 21; *The Terror of the Snows*, by Paul-Marie

Lapointe, trans. D.G. Jones; *Voices from Quebec: An Anthology of Translations*, eds. Philip Stratford and Michael Thomas; *Miror and Letters to an Escapee*, by Roland Giguère, trans. Sheila Fischman; *The Scarecrows of Saint-Emmanuel*, by André Major, trans. Sheila Fischman; *Children of the Black Sabbath*, by Anne Hébert, trans. Carol Dunlop-Hébert; *Garden in the Wind*, by Gabrielle Roy, trans. Alan Brown; *Bitter Bread*, by Albert Laberge, trans. Conrad Dion; *La Duchesse de Langeais and Other Plays*, by Michel Tremblay, trans. John Van Burek; *Sans parachute*, by David Fennario, trans. Gilles Vigneault; and *Sous l'œil de Coyote*, by Sheila Watson, trans. Arlette Francière. *The University of Toronto Quarterly* 47.4 (Summer 1978): 381-395.

Detailed analysis of translations; subjects covered: situation; English-French relations; cultural role; translation of dialogue; dialect; stylistic and lexical errors; treatment of English expressions in translating from French source text; literal translation; *faux amis*; translation of titles; equivalence; retention of French in English translation. ·

298.   O'Connor, John. "Letters in Canada 1978: Translations." Rev. of *Poems of French Canada*, trans. F.R. Scott; *Ellipse* 22; *The Garden of Delights*, by Roch Carrier, trans. Sheila Fischman; *Don Quixote in Nighttown*, by Victor-Lévy Beaulieu, trans. Sheila Fischman; *The Fugitive*, by Marie-Claire Blais, trans. David Lobdell; *Le Lion avait un visage d'homme*, by Robertson Davies, trans. Claire Martin; *Un homme de week-end*, by Richard B. Wright, trans. Jean Paré; and *Out-posts/Avant-postes*, eds. Caroline Bayard and Jack David. *The University of Toronto Quarterly* 48.4 (Summer 1979): 379-394.

Detailed analysis of translations; subjects covered: situation; translation of poetry; literal translation; stylistic errors; problems and difficulties; colloquialisms; retention of French in English translation; lexical errors; translation of titles; equivalence; word play; errors in tone; translation of dialogue; dialect.

299.   O'Connor, John. "Letters in Canada 1979: Translations." Rev. of *The Hockey Sweater and Other Stories*, by Roch Carrier, trans. Sheila Fischman; *The Jimmy Trilogy*, by Jacques Poulin, trans. Sheila Fischman; *Hamlet's Twin*, by Hubert Aquin, trans. Sheila Fischman; *Paris Interlude*, by Naïm Kattan, trans. Sheila Fischman; *A Literary Affair*, by Marie-Claire Blais, trans. Sheila Fischman; *Nights in the Underground: An Exploration of Love*,

by Marie-Claire Blais, trans. Ray Ellenwood; *Wings in the Wind*, by Diane Giguère, trans. Alan Brown; *Children of My Heart*, by Gabrielle Roy, trans. Alan Brown; *La Sagouine*, by Antonine Maillet, trans. Luis de Céspedes; *The Tale of Don l'Orignal*, by Antonine Maillet, trans. Barbara Godard; *Dragon Island*, by Jacques Godbout, trans. David Ellis; *Agoak: The Legacy of Agaguk*, by Yves Thériault, trans. John David Allan; *Creatures of the Chase*, by Jean-Yves Soucy, trans. John Glassco; *The Woman and the Miser*, by Claude-Henri Grignon, trans. Yves Brunelle; *A Collection of Canadian Plays, Volume 7: Seven Authors from Quebec*, ed. Rolf Kalman. *The University of Toronto Quarterly* 49.4 (Summer 1980): 383-399.

Detailed analysis of translations; subjects covered: situation; presence of English expressions in French source text; translation of dialogue; word play; treatment of English expressions in translation from French source text; stylistic, lexical, and grammatical errors; translation of titles; adaptation; English-French relations; capture of style; equivalence; free translation; *faux amis*; problems and difficulties; dialect; colloquialisms; errors in tone; cultural role; political role; editions.

300.   O'Connor, John. "Letters in Canada 1980: Translations." Rev. of *Tales of Solitude*, by Yvette Naubert, trans. Margaret Rose; *Les Stratégies du réel/The Story So Far 6*, ed. Nicole Brossard; *A Québécois Dream*, by Victor-Lévy Beaulieu, trans. Ray Chamberlain; *Salamander: Selected Poems of Robert Marteau*, trans. Jane Winters; *Treatise on White and Tincture*, by Robert Marteau, trans. Barry Callaghan; *Atlante*, by Robert Marteau, trans. Barry Callaghan; *Pentecost*, by Robert Marteau, trans. David Ellis; *The Draft Dodger*, by Louis Caron, trans. David Toby Homel; *Inspector Therrien*, by André Major, trans. Mark Czarnecki; *The Mole Men*, by Négovan Rajic, trans. David Lobdell; *The Ceremony*, by Marie-José Thériault, trans. David Lobdell; *The Umbrella Pines*, by Gilles Archambault, trans. David Lobdell; *Poems by Anne Hébert*, trans. Alfred Poulin, Jr., in *Quarterly Review of Literature* 21.3/4 (1980), Contemporary Poetry Series; *The Agonized Life*, by Gaston Miron, trans. Marc Plourde; *Daydream Mechanics*, by Nicole Brossard, trans. Larry Shouldice; and *The Tin Flute*, by Gabrielle Roy, trans. Alan Brown. *The University of Toronto Quarterly* 50.4 (Summer 1981): 75-95.

Detailed analysis of translations; subjects covered: critics' theories; situation; equivalence; grammatical and lexical errors; errors in tone; treatment of English expressions in translating from French source text; word play; *faux amis*; translation of titles; translation of dialogue; capture of style and tone; gender in translation; ambiguity; publication; linguistic comparison between French and English; author-translator relationship; translation of poetry; colloquialisms; retention of French in English translation; history of translated text.

301. O'Connor, John. "Letters in Canada 1981: Translations." Rev. of *The Rest is Silence*, by Claude Jasmin, trans. David Lobdell; *Eldorado on Ice*, by Denys Chabot, trans. David Lobdell; *Wednesday's Child*, by Gilbert Choquette, trans. David Lobdell; *Contemporary Quebec Criticism*, ed. and trans. Larry Shouldice; *No Country Without Grandfathers*, by Roch Carrier, trans. Sheila Fischman; *The Fat Woman Next Door Is Pregnant*, by Michel Tremblay, trans. Sheila Fischman; *Sainte-Carmen of the Main*, *Damnée Manon, sacrée Sandra*, and *The Impromptu of Outremont*, by Michel Tremblay, trans. John Van Burek; *Entrails*, by Claude Gauvreau, trans. Ray Ellenwood; *The Cart*, by Jacques Ferron, trans. Ray Ellenwood; *Deaf to the City*, by Marie-Claire Blais, trans. Carol Dunlop; and *The Euguélionne: A Triptych Novel*, by Louky Bersianik, trans. Gerry Dennis, Alison Hewitt, Donna Murray, and Martha O'Brien. *The University of Toronto Quarterly* 51.4 (Summer 1982): 391-404.

Detailed analysis of translations; subjects covered: situation; grammatical and lexical errors; literal and faithful translation; translation of titles and dialogue; word play; *faux amis*; retention of French in English translation; colloquialisms, *joual*; capture of style; gender in translation; treatment of English expressions in translating from French source text; presence of English expressions in French source text; policies of the Canada Council.

302. O'Connor, John. "Tremblay's Troupe." Rev. of *The Fat Woman Next Door Is Pregnant*, by Michel Tremblay, trans. Sheila Fischman. Vancouver: Talonbooks, 1981; *The Impromptu of Outremont*, by Michel Tremblay, trans. John Van Burek. Vancouver: Talonbooks, 1981; *Damnée Manon, sacrée Sandra*, by Michel Tremblay, trans. John Van Burek. Vancouver: Talonbooks, 1981; and *Sainte-Carmen of the Main*, by Michel Tremblay, trans. John Van Burek. Vancouver: Talonbooks, 1981. *Canadian Literature* 98 (Autumn 1983): 76-79.

Praises the skill of Fischman's translation but points out certain "weaknesses"; more critical of Van Burek's translation of *The*

Impromptu of Outremont, although acknowledges his skill at translating *joual* and puns; finds the translation of *Damnée Manon, Sacrée Sandra* better, but is critical of *Sainte-Carmen of the Main*. Includes numerous examples of translation problems in all the plays.

303. Patterson, John. F. "Antonine Maillet, traduite ou trahie?" Compte rendu de *The Tale of Don l'Orignal*, par Antonine Maillet, trad. Barbara Godard. Toronto/Vancouver: Clarke Irwin, 1978; et *La Sagouine*, par Antonine Maillet, trad. Luis de Céspedes. Toronto: Simon & Pierre, 1979. *Meta* 28.4 (décembre 1983): 352-357.

Les deux traductions sont très inégales surtout dans la façon dont est rendu l'argot, dans les dialogues et dans la manière dont certaines libertés sont prises; fournit des exemples détaillés et compare des passages de l'original et de la traduction; cependant, Godard est une traductrice plus accomplie.

304. Roht, Toivo. "The Problems and Work of Translators." Rev. of *The Tomb of the Kings*, by Anne Hébert, trans. Peter Miller. Toronto: Contact Press, 1967; and *The King of a Thousand Islands*, by Claude Aubry, trans. Alice Kane. Toronto: McClelland and Stewart, 1963. *Culture* 29.3 (septembre 1968): 254-259.

Discusses the problem of translation as an emblem of the cultural and political relations between French and English Canada; summarizes why there is insufficient literary translation; refers to Patricia Claxton's article in *Meta* [see 280] in relation to the critique that translations in Canada "are simply slavish, unidiomatic renditions which do great injustice to authors and certainly fail to stimulate any interest in the other culture"; mentions cultural and economic conditions and the problems of publishing in Canada; claims that the translation of Hébert's text is "the most important bridge between the two Canadian cultures"; outlines the difficulties faced by the translator and praises the translation as successful; criticizes the translation of Aubry's text, claiming that "the language is often turgid."

305. Seed, Deborah. "Tales to Tantalize." Rev. of *Stories from Quebec*, selected and introduced by Philip Stratford. Toronto: Van Nostrand Reinhold, 1974. *Matrix* 1.1 (Spring 1975): 30-31.

Refers to translation in Canada and the importance of this work; discusses "the problems facing the translators" of the various stories due to *joual*, the "linguistic ingenuity" and particular styles of some Québécois writers; comments on the loss of the original Québécois atmosphere in the process of translation.

306.   Shohet, Linda. "A Shift in Perspective." Rev. of *Allegro*, by Félix Leclerc, trans. Linda Hutcheon. Toronto: McClelland and Stewart, 1974; *Canadians of Old*, by Philippe Aubert de Gaspé, trans. C.G.D. Roberts. Toronto: McClelland and Stewart, 1974. *Journal of Canadian Fiction* 3.4 (1975): 87-89.

Discusses the historical background of the translation of *Canadians of Old*, particularly in terms of the "new Canadian nationalism" fostered by Confederation; mentions the excellent quality of the translation of *Allegro*.

307.   Sloate, Daniel. "Literary Translation: A Few Remarks." Rev. of *Poems by Anne Hébert*, trans. Alan Brown. Don Mills, Ontario: Musson, 1975. *Meta* 21.2 (juin 1976): 165-168.

A lengthy discussion of the processes involved in translation and the translator's role as interpreter—the "subjective intervention" which necessarily occurs, the intensity and quality that "is dependent on the individual translator alone"; uses the term "transcreating" to describe the role of translator as poet; includes several comparative examples and analyses of the subjective choices made by the translator-poet; praises Brown's rendering.

308.   Allen, Antonia. "A Master Storyteller Emerges from Quebec." Rev. of *Tales from the Uncertain Country*, by Jacques Ferron, trans. Betty Bednarski. Toronto: Anansi, 1972. *Saturday Night* 87.8 (August 1973): 37.

Comments on the preservation of Ferron's wit and "feel for the colloquial"; remarks on the usefulness of Bednarski's footnotes to explain "Ferron's own Gallicizing of English words."

309.   Andersen, Margret. Rev. of *The Cart*, by Jacques Ferron, trans. Ray Ellenwood. Toronto: Exile Editions, 1980. *Canadian Book Review Annual* (1981): 132-133.

Describes the state of literary translation in Canada since 1960, explaining why this text was not translated until twelve years after its original publication; claims that Ellenwood "has succeeded in perceiving even the slightest nuance of Ferron's text"; comments on the inevitability of some "linguistic infidelities."

310.   Andrès, Bernard. "Les Surprises d'un *Macbeth* québécois." *Le Devoir* (7 novembre 1978): 17.

L'adaptation de Michel Garneau de "Shakespeare est faite dans une langue drue et savoureuse, puisée artésiennement, comme il le dit 'dans la langue québécoise jusqu'à la source ancestrale.'"

311.   Anonyme. Compte rendu de *Cinquième emploi*, par Robertson Davies, trad. Arlette Francière. Montréal: Le Cercle du Livre de France, 1975. *Le Livre canadien* (octobre 1975): 302.

Critique la traduction qui est "lourde et gauche, émaillée de multiples fautes de français."

312.   Anonyme. Compte rendu de *Telle est ma bien-aimée*, par Morley Callaghan, trad. Michelle Tisseyre. Montréal: Le Cercle du Livre de France, 1974. *Le Livre canadien* (avril 1975): 124.

Critique la traduction sans avoir lu l'original.

313.   Bailey, Bruce. Rev. of *Jack Kerouac: a chicken essay*, by Victor-Lévy Beaulieu, trans. Sheila Fischman. Toronto: Coach House Press, 1975. *Quill & Quire* 42.6 (15 April 1976): 6.

Comments on the skill of Fischman's translation and commends her decision not to translate certain "particularly touching and untranslatable passages in *joual*"; questions Fischman's decision to drop the *accent aigu* from "Kerouac" in the title.

314. Bates, Ronald. Rev. of *Selected Poems*, by Alain Grandbois, trans. Peter Miller. Toronto: Contact Press, 1964. *The Canadian Forum* 45 (July 1965): 95.

Claims that "lyrical poetry is most refractory to translation," and although Peter Miller has done a "workmanlike job," Bates criticizes "the apparently random alternation between use of the genitive case and the genitival 'of.' "

315. Bates, Ronald. Rev. of *St.-Denys Garneau and Anne Hébert*, trans. F.R. Scott. Vancouver: Klanak Press, 1962. *Alphabet* 63.6 (June 1963): 64-65.

Remarks that it is culturally significant "to have good poems in French faced by good translations in English" particularly when "this kind of vis-à-vis dialogue of Canadian culture [is] carried out between three considerable Canadian poets"; claims that Scott's translations convey the rhythm and tone of the originals; refers to the dialogue of Hébert and Scott [see 62]; criticizes Scott's decision to space the lines of Garneau's poetry in order to "bring out the meaning of the phrase."

316. Beaver, John. Rev. of *Angéline de Montbrun*, by Laure Conan, trans. Yves Brunelle. Toronto: University of Toronto Press, 1974. *Quill & Quire* 41.8 (August 1975): 27.

Criticizes the translation as hasty and awkward.

317. Beaver, John. Rev. of *The Silent Rooms*, by Anne Hébert, trans. Kathy Mezei. Don Mills, Ontario: Musson, 1974. *Quill & Quire* 40.12 (December 1974): 22-23.

Claims that the translation conveys the changing nuances of tone.

318. Beaver, John. Rev. of *Tales of Solitude*, by Yvette Naubert, trans. Margaret Rose. Vancouver: Intermedia, 1978. *Quill & Quire* 45.14 (December 1979): 26.

Criticizes the translation, although its failure is attributed in part to the lack of tone and style in the original text; gives one example of a mistranslation.

319. Beaver, John. Rev. of *The Wolf*, by Marie-Claire Blais, trans. Sheila Fischman. Toronto: McClelland and Stewart, 1974. *Quill & Quire* 40.10 (October 1974): 20.

States that this translation will add to Fischman's "growing reputation as a translator" because she has "neatly reproduced the atmosphere" of Blais's text.

320.   Bergeron, Léandre. "Une heureuse initiative." Compte rendu de *St.-Denys Garneau and Anne Hébert*, trans. F.R. Scott. Vancouver: Klanak Press, 1962. *Canadian Literature* 18 (Autumn 1973): 75-76.

La "traduction absolument littérale . . . donne quelquefois du drôle d'anglais mais le respect du poème original qui anime le traducteur excuse facilement ces tournures . . . [et] nous donne vraiment l'impression qu'un Canadien français est en train de nous parler dans sa langue seconde."

321.   Biron, Hervé. Compte rendu du *Matin d'une longue nuit*, par Hugh MacLennan, trad. Jean Simard. Montréal: Éditions HMH, 1967. *Culture* 29.3 (septembre 1978): 271-273.

"La traduction de . . . Simard est excellente . . . [et] fait contraste avec celle des *Deux solitudes* . . . qui ne rend vraiment pas justice à l'ouvrage."

322.   Bourque, Paul-André. Compte rendu des *Poèmes des quatre côtés*, par Jacques Brault. Saint-Lambert: Éditions du Noroît, 1975. *Livres et auteurs québécois*. Québec: Les Presses de l'Université Laval, 1976: 110-112.

Décrit les théories de Brault sur la nontraduction et son processus; commente la façon dont les textes poétiques sont "assez éloignés des originaux de Cummings, Atwood and MacEwen" et "se rapprochent étrangement du Brault de *La Poésie ce matin*," et la manière dont "le poète affirme dans un intertexte, les deux solitudes en même temps que leur impénétrabilité et leur interpénétrabilité" [voir 174].

323.   Bradbury, Maureen. Rev. of *Jack Kerouac: a chicken essay*, by Victor-Lévy Beaulieu, trans. Sheila Fischman. Toronto: Coach House Press, 1975. *Canadian Book Review Annual* (1976): 220-221.

Mentions that the punctuation in the original would present particular problems for the translator and praises the quality of Fischman's rendering.

324.   Bràs, A.R. Rev. of *The Insecurity of Art*, eds. Ken Norris and Peter Van Toorn. Montreal: Véhicule Press, 1982. *Rubicon* 1 (Spring 1983): 118-120.

Comments on articles by D.G. Jones [see 70], Marc Plourde [see 252], and F.R. Scott [see 258]; focusses on Plourde's piece claiming that he "illustrates the difficulty of rendering into another language . . . the work of a poet of Gaston Miron's complexity."

325. Brissenden, Connie. "Up the New!" Rev. of *The Cry of the Whippoorwill*, by Guy Dufresne, trans. Philip London and Laurence Bérard. Toronto: New Press, 1972; *The White Geese*, by Marcel Dubé, trans. Jean Remple. Toronto: New Press, 1972; and *The Hanged Man*, by Robert Gurik, trans. Philip London and Laurence Bérard. Toronto: New Press, 1972. *Canadian Literature* 59 (Winter 1974): 111-113.

Criticizes the translation of Dufresne and Dubé as tedious and aggravating; the translation of Gurik's text, in contrast, is praised as an honest and sensitive rendering of the original script.

326. Carpenter, David. "Conte and Memoir." Rev. of *Selected Tales of Jacques Ferron*, trans. Betty Bednarski. Toronto: Anansi, 1984. *Canadian Literature* 108 (Spring 1986): 165-169.

Discusses the inadequacy of certain anglophone expressions in communicating the specific connotations of the French—"the myriad nuances of Québec life embedded in Ferron's prose."

327. Carrier, Jean-Guy. "The One-Eyed Ambassadors." Rev. of *Poems of French Canada*, trans. F.R. Scott. Burnaby, B.C.: Blackfish Press, 1975; and *The Poetry of Modern Quebec*, trans. Fred Cogswell. Montreal: Harvest House, 1976. *Books in Canada* 6 (October 1977): 23.

Praises Scott's translation in particular and compares the "individual approaches to translation" of Scott and Cogswell.

328. Clark, Matthew. "In the Shadow of the Wind." Rev. of *In the Shadow of the Wind*, by Anne Hébert, trans. Sheila Fischman. Toronto: Stoddard, 1983. *Quill & Quire* 49.11 (November 1983): 20.

Comments on the skill of Fischman's translation, which "does justice to the faults of Hébert's prose."

329. Cloutier, Cécile. "A Way of Loving." Rev. of *The Journal of Saint-Denys Garneau*, trans. John Glassco. Toronto: McClelland and Stewart, 1962. *Evidence* 9 (c1965): 118-120.

Discusses the difficulty of translating and of capturing the essence of an individual's personal expression; considers Glassco's work "honest."

330. Cloutier, Pierre. Rev. of *A Second Hundred Poems of Modern Quebec*, ed. and trans. Fred Cogswell. Fredericton: Fiddlehead Poetry Books, 1971. *Quarry* 22.2 (Spring 1973): 74-75.

Emphasis of review is on the translation; comments on the importance of translation to "cross-cultural communication in this country"; presents Cogswell's translations as "fine, sometimes extremely well done."

331. Cogswell, Fred. Rev. of *The Poetry of French Canada in Translation*, ed. John Glassco. Toronto: Oxford University Press, 1970. *Fiddlehead* 88 (Winter 1971): 103-104.

States that he agrees with Glassco's "theory of translation as he sets down in his introduction" [see 227], but goes on to outline his own views on translation and what kind of work he considers to be "only half translations"—work that has failed to be sensitive to the rhythm and diction of the original; calls this anthology a work of "flawed heroism"; and comments on each of the translator's renderings.

332. Cogswell, Fred. Rev. of *Selected Poems of Émile Nelligan*, trans. P.F. Widdows. Toronto: The Ryerson Press, 1960. *Fiddlehead* 48 (Spring 1961): 53.

Praises translations and quotes Widdows's version of "Devant le feu" as illustrating his skill better than any words could do.

333. Cogswell, Fred. Rev. of *Stories from Quebec*, selected and introduced by Philip Stratford. Toronto: Van Nostrand Reinhold, 1974. *Queen's Quarterly* 83.1 (Spring 1976): 171-172.

Compares the translation of short stories with poetry in terms of the "loss of tonal and emotional richness"; also comments on the increase in translations and the benefit to "future relations between the two cultures."

334. Cook, Ramsay. "Acadian Odyssey." Rev. of *Pélagie*, by Antonine Maillet, trans. Philip Stratford. Garden City, New York: Doubleday and Co., 1982. *Saturday Night* 97.3 (March 1982): 54-55.

Praises the translation because Stratford has rendered the "colloquial flavour without even a hint of the W.H. Drummond-like condescension that sometimes creeps into translations of popular speech."

335. Cowan, Hector. "Thériault's Lament." Rev. of *Ashini*, by Yves Thériault, trans. Gwendolyn Moore. Montreal: Harvest House,

1972; and *N'Tsuk*, by Yves Thériault, trans. Gwendolyn Moore. Montreal: Harvest House, 1971. *Canadian Literature* 59 (Winter 1974): 125-126.

Comments on the accessibility of the texts to translation; although Moore's rendering is generally good, there is some criticism of "her use of excessively literal terms."

336. Cowan, Judith. Rev. of *Selected Tales of Jacques Ferron*, trans. Betty Bednarski. Toronto: Anansi, 1984. *Matrix* 20 (Spring 1985): 72-75.

States that the translation is "fluent and easy to read"; discusses the difficulty of translating Ferron because of his innovative style; gives a few examples of translation flaws; and compares a passage in the source and target text.

337. Czarnecki, Mark. "The Chronicles of Michel Tremblay, part II." Rev. of *Thérèse and Pierrette and the Little Hanging Angel*, by Michel Tremblay, trans. Sheila Fischman. Toronto: McClelland and Stewart, 1984. *Quill & Quire* 50.6 (June 1984): 30.

Comments on difficulty of translating *joual* and claims that Fischman's rendering is too formal in the social context; also mentions a minor omission in the translation of the title.

338. Dagenais, Gérard. "Jean Simard ou les difficultés de la traduction." Compte rendu du *Temps tournera au beau*, par Hugh MacLennan, trad. Jean Simard. Montréal: Éditions HMH, 1966. *Nos écrivains et le français*. Montréal: Éditions du Jour, 1967. 93-101.

Expose rapidement ses théories sur la traduction (qui devrait être idéalement une interprétation, une transposition, sans trahison); démontre à l'aide d'exemples détaillés la qualité de la traduction de Jean Simard; souligne certains problèmes que pose l'utilisation par ce dernier d'anglicismes stylistiques et linguistiques.

339. Dansereau, Estelle. Rev. of *The Agonized Life*, by Gaston Miron, trans. Marc Plourde. Montreal: Torchy Wharf Press, 1980. *Quarry* 30.1 (Winter 1981): 79-82.

Discusses the art of translating and the responsibilities of the translator to capture the nuances of the original. Criticizes Plourde's translations as "only marginally successful," and provides numerous examples demonstrating how the translations fail to reflect the spirit of Miron's text.

340. Dansereau, Estelle. Rev. of *Broke City*, by Jacques Renaud, trans. David Homel. Montreal: Guernica Editions, 1984; and *Embers and Earth: Selected Poems*, by Gaston Miron, trans. D.G. Jones and Marc Plourde. Montreal: Guernica Editions, 1984. *Quarry* 35.3 (Summer 1986): 103-107.

Comments in detail on Homel's equivalent form for *joual* in *Broke City* which is a "suitable version of proletarian discourse, but one which does not convey the sense of place"; states that Homel succeeds in "translating the down-and-out's anger and frustration"; Plourde's translations in *Embers and Earth* are not as effective as D.G. Jones's.

341. Dansereau, Estelle. Rev. of *Eldorado on Ice*, by Denys Chabot, trans. David Lobdell. Ottawa: Oberon Press, 1981. *Quarry* 31 (Spring 1982): 86-90.

Comments on the recent increase in the translation of Québécois writing and discusses the translation of this novel at length; praises Lobdell's work because he has captured certain aspects of the tone and style of the original, such as the baroque effect; provides one substantial comparative example of Lobdell's skill, and numerous brief examples of minor flaws.

342. Dansereau, Estelle. Rev. of *Letter by Letter*, by Louise Maheux-Forcier, trans. David Lobdell. Ottawa: Oberon Press, 1982. *Quarry* 33.3 (Summer 1984): 88-91.

Claims that the stories "have been skilfully translated . . . and convey, for the most part, her not inconsiderable stylistic flair"; refers to Lobdell's introductory "Translator's Note" [see 239].

343. Dassylva, Martial. "Ce 'Macbeth' qui est d'abord de William Shakespeare et ensuite de Michel Garneau." *La Presse* (28 octobre 1978): D4.

"Cette traduction . . . représente un geste politique en ce sens qu'on assume Shakespeare comme dramaturge anglais et qu'on assume, par la traduction, la langue québécoise . . . la traduction en français la plus belle que j'ai jamais vue."

344. Davies, Gillian. Rev. of *Between Crows and Indians*, by Roger Magini, trans. Marc Plourde. Toronto: Coach House Press, 1976. *Fiddlehead* 117 (Spring 1978): 143-149.

Lists a number of examples of errors in "structure and preposition, etc.," which may be the fault of Coach House Press or because Plourde is not an anglophone.

345. Davies, Gillian. "Les Confitures de coing." Rev. of *Quince Jam*, by Jacques Ferron, trans. Ray Ellenwood. Toronto: Coach House Press, 1977. *Brick: A Journal of Reviews* 4 (Fall 1978): 53-54.

Discusses the translation of Ferron's books in general as well as this translation in particular; notes Ellenwood's skill in rendering Ferron's often subtle language; also mentions a few minor faults.

346. Davies, Gillian. "De bouche en oreille." Rev. of *La Sagouine*, by Antonine Maillet, trans. Luis de Céspedes. Toronto: Simon & Pierre, 1979. *Brick: A Journal of Reviews* 10 (Fall 1980): 23-24. Rpt. 12 (Spring 1981): 70-71.

Describes Céspedes's successful rendition, methodology, and style.

347. Davies, Gillian. Rev. of *Dürer's Angel*, by Marie-Claire Blais, trans. David Lobdell. Vancouver: Talonbooks, 1976. *Fiddlehead* 114 (Summer 1977): 147-149.

Praises the translation as exemplary; provides one example of how Lobdell has captured the *"gaucherie* of the original."

348. Davies, Gillian. Rev. of *The Fugitive*, by Marie-Claire Blais, trans. David Lobdell. Ottawa: Oberon Press, 1978. *Fiddlehead* 121 (Spring 1979): 163-164.

Discusses Lobdell's translation of the title in terms of how it widens the scope of the original; lists a number of "creative liberties" taken with the source text, resulting in a translation that is less fervent in tone.

349. Davies, Gillian. Rev. of *Stories from Quebec*, selected and introduced by Philip Stratford. Toronto: Van Nostrand Reinhold, 1974. *Fiddlehead* 106 (Summer 1975): 117-120.

Considers most of the translations to be excellent, but claims that some of the stories likely posed problems—"it is probably the innovators with language who provide the most difficulties for their translators"; mentions the translation of Marie-Claire Blais by Vida Bruce, of Réjean Ducharme by William Kinsley, and of Jacques Renaud by Ronald Bates.

350. Davies, Gillian. Rev. of *The Tale of Don l'Orignal*, by Antonine Maillet, trans. Barbara Godard. Toronto: Clarke Irwin, 1978. *Fiddlehead* 124 (Winter 1980): 135-138.

Outlines the use of vernacular speech in the French text and praises Godard's rendering of this and of the swear words; claims that the translation captures the spirit of the original.

351. Davies, Gillian. Rev. of *Tales from the Uncertain Country*, by Jacques Ferron, trans. Betty Bednarski. Toronto: Anansi, 1972. *Fiddlehead* 110 (Summer 1976): 134-137.

    Comments on what is paramount to the art of translation, the idiosyncratic nature of Ferron's style, and Bednarski's textual explanation of some typical Ferron neologisms.

352. Davies, Gillian. Rev. of *The Wolf*, by Marie-Claire Blais, trans. Sheila Fischman. Toronto: McClelland and Stewart, 1974; and *St. Lawrence Blues*, by Marie-Claire Blais, trans. Ralph Manheim. New York: Farrar, Straus & Giroux, 1974. *Fiddlehead* 104 (Winter 1975): 128-131.

    Acknowledges that *The Wolf* would be difficult to translate because of the "length and intricacy of Blais's sentences," and points out some weaknesses in Fischman's translation. Because of the prevalence of *joual*, discusses Manheim's translation in more detail, and indicates instances where the idiom is inadequately rendered.

353. Delisle, Jean. Compte rendu de *Dialogue sur la traduction*, par Anne Hébert et Frank Scott. Montréal: Éditions HMH, 1970. *Meta* 20.3 (septembre 1975): 228-229.

    Description du "Dialogue" et discussion sur la façon dont "la traduction, loin de dénaturer ou travestir un poème, lui donne un nouveau visage" [voir 176].

354. De Vries, Bert. Rev. of *Les Belles Sœurs*, by Michel Tremblay, trans. John Van Burek and Bill Glassco. Vancouver: Talonbooks, 1974. *Quarry* 25.1 (Winter 1976): 77-79.

    Praises the translation, which "very deftly handles the knotty problem of rendering *joual* into English"; explains why *joual* cannot be translated "word for word"; also comments on the non-translation of "French-Canadian swearing . . . which, if literally translated . . . loses all its rich cadences and expressiveness."

355. Downes, Gwladys V. "Hébert in English." Rev. of *Poems by Anne Hébert*, trans. Alan Brown. Don Mills, Ontario: Musson, 1975. *Canadian Literature* 71 (Winter 1976): 87-89.

    Includes a general discussion of translation; explains that poetry is more difficult to translate than prose; discusses Brown's translations in detail, noting the flaws.

356. Downes, Gwladys V. "Inconsistencies." Rev. of *The Complete Poems of Émile Nelligan*, trans. Fred Cogswell. Montreal: Harvest House, 1983. *Canadian Literature* 102 (Autumn 1984): 153-154.

Detailed critique of these translations, pointing out the inconsistencies and incongruities between the tone and intent of the source and target texts.

357. Dragland, Stan. Rev. of *The Complete Poems of Saint-Denys Garneau*, trans. and ed. John Glassco. Ottawa: Oberon Press, 1975. *Quarry* 25.4 (Autumn 1976): 76-80.

Discusses the desirability that the translator disappear in the translation, comments on Glassco's success in achieving this; quotes from Glassco's theories on translation in his introduction to *The Poetry of French Canada in Translation* [see 227].

358. Dudek, Louis. Rev. of *Selected Poems of Émile Nelligan*, trans. P.F. Widdows. Toronto: The Ryerson Press, 1960. *The Canadian Forum* 41 (July 1961): 92.

Calls the translations feeble and gives an illustrative example.

359. Eccles, W.J. Rev. of *Word from New France: The Selected Letters of Marie de l'Incarnation*, trans. and ed. Joyce Marshall. Toronto: Oxford University Press, 1967. *Canadian Historical Review* 49.2 (June 1968): 171-173.

Judges translation favourably, although it is occasionally too literal.

360. Ellenwood, [William] Ray. "Artist's Angel." Rev. of *Dürer's Angel*, by Marie-Claire Blais, trans. David Lobdell. Vancouver: Talonbooks, 1976. *Open Letter* 3.8 (Spring 1978): 118-120.

Comments on the difficulty of translating Blais's dialogue, and on the stilted quality of the English version.

361. Ellenwood, [William] Ray. "Broad Study." Rev. of *Surrealism and Quebec Literature: History of a Cultural Revolution*, by André G. Bourassa, trans. Mark Czarnecki. Toronto: University of Toronto Press, 1984. *Brick: A Journal of Reviews* 23 (Winter 1985): 42-44.

Claims that "the translated version is an improvement on the original in a number of ways"; comments on the extensive translator's notes that "help explain Bourassa's allusions, giving bits of information a Québécois reader would take for granted";

discusses the "expertise and/or research" necessarily undertaken by the translator of this kind of text, and the decision made by Czarnecki for complete "anglification."

362. Ellenwood, [William] Ray. "You! borduas." Rev. of *Écrits/Writings 1942-1958*, by Paul-Émile Borduas. Présentés et édités par/Introduced and edited by François-Marc Gagnon. Trad./trans. François-Marc Gagnon and Dennis Young. Halifax: The Nova Scotia College of Art and Design, 1978. *Brick: A Journal of Reviews* 13 (Fall 1981): 5-7.

Comments on the difficulty of translating this work, the overall success of the translation, and on the occasionally too literal rendering.

363. Everett, Jane. Rev. of *The Madman, the Kite and the Island*, by Félix Leclerc, trans. Philip Stratford. Ottawa: Oberon Press, 1976. *Quarry* 26.4 (Autumn 1977): 74-76.

Claims that Stratford's translation conveys the "atmosphere . . . typical of Leclerc's work"; questions why the translator omitted part of the original text, thus making the novel more ambiguous.

364. Fischman, Sheila. Rev. of *Hail Galarneau!*, by Jacques Godbout, trans. Alan Brown. Toronto: Longman Canada, 1970. *The Globe Magazine* (19 December 1970): 16.

Mentions that Brown and Godbout are given the same attention on the book's cover, which is justified because "Alan Brown's translation is a true recreation of Jacques Godbout's very fine and technically difficult novel, and if translation is to be recognized (as it should be) as an honest craft, that recognition should come first of all from the people who publish translations."

365. Fischman, Sheila. "In Praise of Younger Men." Rev. of *Children of My Heart*, by Gabrielle Roy, trans. Alan Brown. Toronto: McClelland and Stewart, 1979. *Books in Canada* 8.5 (May 1979): 17-18.

Comments on the excellent quality of the translation and how Brown has captured Roy's style while remaining, "quite properly, invisible."

366. Foran, Charles. Rev. of *Selected Tales of Jacques Ferron*, trans. Betty Bednarski. Toronto: Anansi, 1985. *Rubicon* 6 (Winter 1985/ 86): 168-169.

Claims that Bednarski "displays a necessary sensitivity to the peculiarities of Ferron's language . . . with a less able translator many of these nuances might have been lost."

367. Frank, Anne. "Two Quebec Playwrights." Rev. of *Les Belles Sœurs*, by Michel Tremblay, trans. John Van Burek and Bill Glassco. Vancouver: Talonbooks, 1974. *The Tamarack Review* 68 (Spring 1976): 86-89.

Comments on the change of focus in the translation and the loss of "political overtones."

368. Garebian, Keith. "Trash, Tinsel and Two Jewels." Rev. of *Forever Yours, Marie-Lou*, by Michel Tremblay, trans. John Van Burek and Bill Glassco. Vancouver: Talonbooks, 1975; and *Hosanna*, by Michel Tremblay, trans. John Van Burek and Bill Glassco. Vancouver: Talonbooks, 1974. *Performing Arts in Canada* 15.3 (Fall 1978): 35-36.

A review of the theatrical productions of these plays; in *Forever Yours, Marie-Lou* "the dramatic elements don't mix in English translation" because of the prevalence of *joual*. The production of *Hosanna* is more successful because it "transcends its flaws."

369. Garebian, Keith. "Trite Parable." Rev. of *The Garden of Delights*, by Roch Carrier, trans. Sheila Fischman. Toronto: Anansi, 1978. *Canadian Literature* 88 (Spring 1981): 98-100.

Comments on the difficulty of translating the "emblematic puns," and criticizes Fischman's translation as "lumpy literalism."

370. Gerson, Carole. "Shot-gun Fiction." Rev. of *The Scarecrows of Saint-Emmanuel*, by André Major, trans. Sheila Fischman. Toronto: McClelland and Stewart, 1977. *Essays on Canadian Writing* 9 (Winter 1977/78): 147-149.

Suggests that "some of this novel's superficiality may be due to the difficulty of finding an English equivalent for *joual*"; questions Fischman's decision to anglicize a number of the names and to change the "scarecrow" of the title from the singular to the plural.

371. Gibson, Shirley. "Langevin: Something Lost in Translation." Rev. of *Orphan Street*, by André Langevin, trans. Alan Brown. Toronto: McClelland and Stewart, 1976. *Saturday Night* 91.8 (November 1976): 56-58.

Criticizes the translation and apparent lack of good editing; remarks on the awkwardness of the language, and on the lack of subtlety and precision in the translation of idiom and expletives.

372. Giguère, Richard. Compte rendu de *La Traduction poétique*. Numéro spécial de *Meta* 23.1 (mars 1978). *Canadian Review of Comparative Literature/Revue canadienne de littérature comparée* 9.1 (March 1982): 124-128.

"L'ensemble des articles est représentatif . . . de l'état de la traduction littéraire non seulement au Québec et au Canada, mais aux États-Unis et en Europe." Déclare que, comme *Meta* publie relativement peu sur la traduction littéraire, c'est un numéro important.

373. Godard, Barbara. Rev. of *The Antiphonary*, by Hubert Aquin, trans. Alan Brown. Toronto: Anansi, 1973. *The Canadian Forum* 53 (November/December 1973): 33-34.

Comments on how the "Aquinian neologisms" are translated; praises Brown's rendering of the novel's "rhythms, colour and precision."

374. Godard, Barbara. "Ferron's Magical Ark." Rev. of *Dr. Cotnoir*, by Jacques Ferron, trans. Pierre Cloutier. Montreal: Harvest House, 1973. *Journal of Canadian Fiction* 3.2 (1974): 107-108.

Although Cloutier's translation is "generally excellent," Godard discusses the difficulty of translating Ferron's language and the failure of the translation to capture certain nuances of the original; gives some examples of the heaviness of Cloutier's translation when compared to Ferron's "rapier-like original."

375. Godard, Barbara. "Kamouraska." Rev. of *Kamouraska*, by Anne Hébert, trans. Norman Shapiro. Don Mills, Ontario: Musson, 1973. *Open Letter* 2.6 (Fall 1973): 121-123.

States that the translation is "a brilliantly inspired one"; also includes two instances where the translator goes beyond Hébert's text and assumes "the writer's role."

376. Godard, Barbara. "Quebec Theatre." Rev. of *The White Geese*, by Marcel Dubé, trans. Jean Remple. Toronto: New Press, 1972; *The Cry of the Whippoorwill*, by Guy Dufresne, trans. Philip London and Laurence Bérard. Toronto: New Press, 1972; and *The Hanged Man*, by Robert Gurik, trans. Philip London and Laurence Bérard.

Toronto: New Press, 1972. *Open Letter* 2.7 (Spring 1974): 86-91.

Provides an overview of the translation of French-Canadian drama in terms of previous translations; discusses the scarcity of translation and the motivation for publishing the plays in translation. Comments on the adequate quality of translation in the three texts reviewed but points out numerous oddities and flaws—the uncalled-for change in names, some instances of "general sloppiness" and "more serious distortions," and the poor rendering of swear words in Gurik's play.

377. Godard, Barbara. Rev. of *The Rope Dancer*, by Wilfrid Lemoine, trans. David Lobdell. Ottawa: Oberon Press, 1979. *Fiddlehead* 123 (Fall 1979): 116-117.

Although it "reads well in English," it "is marred by the occasional omission, or . . . by the translator's yielding to the temptation to render in correct grammatical sentences some of the fleeting impressions—stream-of-consciousness-like—which give the monologue its flavour."

378. Godard, Barbara. Rev. of *La Sagouine*, by Antonine Maillet, trans. Luis de Céspedes. Toronto: Simon & Pierre, 1979. *Quill & Quire* 45.8 (July 1979): 47-48.

Claims that a comparison of the sketch "The Census" with two other translations reveals that this rendering does not fully rise "to the challenge"; while the "theatrical experience remains in the translation," the "linguistic comedy" is lost; gives one example, comparing this version to Stratford's, which "goes straight to the point."

379. Godard, Barbara. Rev. of *St. Lawrence Blues*, by Marie-Claire Blais, trans. Ralph Manheim. New York: Farrar, Straus & Giroux, 1974. *Quill & Quire* 41.1 (January 1975): 23-24.

Criticizes the inadequate translation of *joual* and the consequent loss of "punch" and "parody" of the original.

380. Godard, Barbara. Rev. of *Tales from the Uncertain Country*, by Jacques Ferron, trans. Betty Bednarski. Toronto: New Press, 1972; and *Tales sur la pointe des pieds*, by Gilles Vigneault, trans. Paul Allard. Erin, Ontario: Press Porcépic, 1972. *Open Letter* 2.3 (Fall 1972): 93-97.

Discussion of translation focusses on Ferron's book: the benefit of Bednarski's translation notes, the difficulty of Ferron's language; some criticism of the translations because they do not capture the lyrical flavour of the originals.

381. Godard, Barbara. Rev. of *Translation in Canadian Literature: Symposium 1982*. Reappraisals: Canadian Writers 9, ed. Camille R. La Bossière. Ottawa: University of Ottawa Press, 1983. *The University of Toronto Quarterly* 53.4 (Summer 1984): 500-502.

Describes how the essays, several of which describe the political realities of translation in Canada, confirm her impression that translation in Canada is still a discrete and unorganized activity, particularly in theory.

382. Godard, Barbara. "Visionary." Rev. of *Atlante*, by Robert Marteau, trans. Barry Callaghan. Bilingual Edition. Toronto: Exile Editions, 1979; and *Traité du blanc et des teintures/Treatise on White and Tincture*, by Robert Marteau, trans. Barry Callaghan. Bilingual Edition. Toronto: Exile Editions, 1980. *Brick: A Journal of Reviews* 14 (Winter 1982): 48-49.

Discusses the difficulty of translating sounds, specifically alliteration, in poetry.

383. Godard, Barbara. "Why Things Happen." Rev. of *The Scarecrows of Saint-Emmanuel*, by André Major, trans. Sheila Fischman. Toronto: McClelland and Stewart, 1977. *Waves* 6.3: 77-79.

Praises the translation as it errs "neither in its literalness nor in its liberty with the original structures"; claims that Fischman's rendering endows the style with "additional force."

384. Godard, Barbara. Rev. of *Wings in the Wind*, by Diane Giguère, trans. Alan Brown. Toronto: McClelland and Stewart, 1979. *Quill & Quire* 45.3 (16 February 1979): 15.

Comments on the translation's capture of the "poetry of the original" and the "subtle shift in style" between the two sections of the novel; also mentions the adaptation of imagery associations.

385. Grosskurth, Phyllis. "Vapour from a Jewelled Casket." Rev. of *The Silent Rooms*, by Anne Hébert, trans. Kathy Mezei. Don Mills, Ontario: Musson, 1974. *Canadian Literature* 65 (Summer 1975): 117-118.

Comments on the art of translation and the difficulty of conveying mood—"what may be grand in French becomes grandiose in

English"; gives examples of a number of "solecisms"; mentions the number of translation flaws in Anne Hébert's *Kamouraska* and in "Hannah Josephson's embarrassing translation of Gabrielle Roy's *Bonheur d'occasion.*"

386. Grube, John. "Le Chemin de Ferron." Rev. of *Dr. Cotnoir*, by Jacques Ferron, trans. Pierre Cloutier. Montreal: Harvest House, 1973; and *The Saint-Elias*, by Jacques Ferron, trans. Pierre Cloutier. Montreal: Harvest House, 1975. *Books in Canada* 4.1 (January 1975): 8-9.

Comments on the importance of Ferron's style and on the necessity of capturing his style in the translation; contrasts the two translations by Cloutier, and claims that *The Saint-Elias* is superior to *Dr. Cotnoir* because Ferron's style is captured more successfully.

387. Gruslin, Adrien. "Le *Macbeth* de Garneau." *Le Devoir* (10 mars 1979): 29.

Compte rendu de l'adaptation québécoise du *Macbeth* de Michel Garneau: "la parlure de l'auteur . . . a ses règles puisées dans un français d'hier, vieilli, revampé par le labeur minutieux de l'écrivain-poète."

388. Hainer, R.C. Rev. of *Kamouraska*, by Anne Hébert, trans. Norman Shapiro. Don Mills, Ontario: Musson, 1973. *English Quarterly* 7.4 (Winter 1974/75): 89-92.

Praises the translation for capturing the tone and intensity of the original; criticizes instances where "the verbs are weak and the sense literal."

389. Hancock, Geoff. "Styx and Stones." Rev. of *The Cart*, by Jacques Ferron, trans. Ray Ellenwood. Toronto: Exile Editions, 1980. *Books in Canada* 11.2 (February 1982): 14-15.

Notes that "the narrative starts getting rather muddled, and without Ray Ellenwood's notes doesn't always make sense."

390. Hathorn, Ramon. "Ferron, Fiction and Philosophy." Rev. of *The Juneberry Tree*, by Jacques Ferron, trans. Ray Chamberlain. Montreal: Harvest House, 1975. *Journal of Canadian Fiction* 17/ 18 (1976): 312-314.

Praises the translation, particularly Chamberlain's rendering of Ferron's style and his use of textual notes to explain Ferronian puns; provides some examples of the "appropriate liberties" taken in the translation, as well as of a few translation flaws.

391. Hayne, David M. "Aggressive Individualist." Rev. of *Convergence: Essays from Quebec*, by Jean Le Moyne, trans. Philip Stratford. Toronto: The Ryerson Press, 1966. *Canadian Literature* 32 (Spring 1967): 77-78.

Praises this translation of a difficult work and lists a number of examples of minor mistranslations.

392. Hayne, David M. Rev. of *Bibliography of Canadian Books in Translation: French to English and English to French/Bibliographie de livres canadiens traduits de l'anglais au français et du français à l'anglais*, by/par Philip Stratford and/et Maureen Newman. Prepared for The Committee on Translation of the Humanities Research Council of Canada/préparé pour le Comité de la traduction du Conseil canadien de recherches sur les humanités. Ottawa: Humanities Research Council of Canada/Conseil canadien de recherches sur les humanités, 1975. Second edition/deuxième édition. Ottawa: HRCC/CCRH, 1977. *Papers of the Bibliographical Society of Canada/Cahiers de la Société bibliographique du Canada* 17 (1978): 78-79.

Outlines the usefulness of the bibliography despite a few inconsistencies.

393. Hayne, David [M]. "A Poet's Diary." Rev. of *The Journal of Saint-Denys Garneau*, trans. John Glassco. Toronto: McClelland and Stewart, 1962. *Canadian Literature* 17 (Summer 1963): 67-68.

Praises the translation at length, claiming that "even those who can read the *Journal* in French will profit from Mr. Glassco's helpful renderings"; lists several examples of minor mistranslations.

394. Heller, Liane. "A Masterful Gallery of Acadian Rogues." Rev. of *The Devil is Loose!*, by Antonine Maillet, trans. Philip Stratford. Toronto: Lester & Orpen Dennys, 1986. *Maclean's* 99.21 (26 May 1986): 52.

Claims that the novel is brilliantly translated, because the author's distinctive use of Acadian idioms is reflected by Stratford's "French-accented Elizabethan English."

395. Hind-Smith, Joan. Rev. of *Children of My Heart*, by Gabrielle Roy, trans. Alan Brown. Toronto: McClelland and Stewart, 1979. *Quill & Quire* 45.5 (April 1979): 29.

Criticizes the non-translation of the stories' titles, claiming that this is a loss.

396.   Hind-Smith, Joan. "Joualling with Joyce." Rev. of *Don Quixote in Nighttown*, by Victor-Lévy Beaulieu, trans. Sheila Fischman. Erin, Ontario: Press Porcépic, 1978. *Books in Canada* 7 (June/July 1978): 17.

Comments on the difficulties of translating puns, *joual*, and idiom; claims that Fischman's rendering is "handled so smoothly the book reads as though it had originally been written in English."

397.   Holland, Patrick. Rev. of *The Poetry of Modern Quebec: An Anthology*, ed. and trans. Fred Cogswell. Montreal: Harvest House, 1976. *Canadian Book Review Annual* (1976): 191.

Claims that "this anthology inevitably demands comparison with John Glassco's *The Poetry of French Canada in Translation . . .* an anthology which has already achieved classic status"; Cogswell's anthology "will not easily supplant John Glassco's earlier work"; comments on the "wooden" quality of the translations.

398.   Homel, David [Toby]. "Antonine Maillet's Eternal Return of the Acadian Character." Rev. of *The Devil is Loose!*, by Antonine Maillet, trans. Philip Stratford. Toronto: Lester & Orpen Dennys, 1986. *Quill & Quire* 52.6 (June 1986): 39.

Mentions Stratford's consultation with Maillet in connection with this translation and that of *Pélagie* (1982), and the resulting liberal rendition.

399.   Homel, David Toby. "On the Road to Nowhere." Rev. of *The Rope Dancer*, by Wilfrid Lemoine, trans. David Lobdell. Ottawa: Oberon Press, 1979. *Books in Canada* 8.7 (August/September 1979): 21-22.

Discusses the translator's duty to select books worthy of translation, and questions why this text was chosen.

400.   Homel, David [Toby]. "Silhouettes on the Shade." Rev. of *Best Man*, by Claire Martin, trans. David Lobdell. Ottawa: Oberon Press, 1983. *Books in Canada* 12.7 (August/September, 1983): 29.

Questions why this novel was translated and certain decisions by the translator.

401. Hornbeck, Paul. Rev. of *Farewell, Babylon*, by Naïm Kattan, trans.
Sheila Fischman. Toronto: McClelland and Stewart, 1976. *Quill
& Quire* 42.14 (18 October 1976): 7-8.

Comments on the skill of the translation because it catches "the
Iraqi mood of the author's original French."

402. Houde, Roland. "L'Œuvre en traduction." Compte rendu de *Bibliography of Canadian Books in Translation: French to English and
English to French/Bibliographie de livres canadiens traduits de
l'anglais au français et du français à l'anglais*, by/par Philip
Stratford and/et Maureen Newman. Prepared for the Committee
on Translation of the Humanities Research Council of Canada/
préparé pour le Comité de la traduction du Conseil canadien de
recherches sur les humanitiés. Ottawa: Humanities Research Council of Canada/Conseil canadien de recherches sur les humanités,
1975. *Meta* 23.3 (septembre 1978): 220-225.

Cite l'abbé Arthur Maheux et l'abbé Lionel Groulx quant à
l'importance de la traduction au Canada; mentionne quelques
traducteurs et l'histoire de certaines associations spécialisées;
marque son désaccord sur le titre et les catégories; énumère
omissions et erreurs.

403. Issenhurth, Jean-Pierre. "Blind Painting." Compte rendu de *Blind
Painting*, by Robert Melançon, trans. Philip Stratford. Montreal:
Signal Editions, 1986. *Liberté* 165 (juin 1986): 138-141.

Indique que la traduction de Stratford rend bien "le mouvement
perpétuel, sans ruptures" de Melançon, mais signale les particu-
larités rythmiques que "l'anglais escamote," et le fait que des
mots qui reviennent souvent sont traduits différemment, ce qui
rend plus vague le thème de Melançon.

404. Jones, D.G. Rev. of *The Complete Poems of Saint-Denys Garneau*,
trans. and ed. John Glassco. Ottawa: Oberon Press, 1975. *Queen's
Quarterly* 83.4 (Winter 1976): 694-695.

Claims that Glassco has captured the spirit of the originals;
compares Glassco's approach to Garneau with Scott's, although
views both translators favourably; gives a number of examples of
translation flaws: expressions that are slightly archaic, odd, or
that have been over-interpreted.

405. Jones, D.G. Rev. of *Poems by Anne Hébert*, trans. Alan Brown.
Don Mills, Ontario: Musson, 1975. *Queen's Quarterly* 85.1
(Spring 1978): 151-152.

Discusses the difficulty of translating much of French-Canadian poetry into English because "it may lose resonance"; compares Brown's translation of Hébert with Scott's; includes a number of examples of minor mistranslations.

406. Kingstone, Basil. "Lunar Provinces." Rev. of *Moon Country*, by Denys Chabot, trans. David Lobdell. Ottawa: Oberon Press, 1984. *The Canadian Forum* 64 (October 1985): 31-32.

Lists several oddities in the translation, but claims that the text seldom reminds one that it is not the original.

407. Kingstone, Basil. Rev. of *The Silent Rooms*, by Anne Hébert, trans. Kathy Mezei. Don Mills, Ontario: Musson, 1974. *University of Windsor Review* 10.2 (Spring/Summer 1975): 86-87.

Discusses the failure of the translation to consistently render the poetic structure of Hébert's text; gives numerous examples of flaws and good points.

408. Kirley, Kevin. "French Writers of Canada." Rev. of *The Juneberry Tree*, by Jacques Ferron, trans. Ray Chamberlain. Montreal: Harvest House, 1975; *The Saint-Elias*, by Jacques Ferron, trans. Pierre Cloutier. Montreal: Harvest House, 1975; and *Jos Carbone*, by Jacques Benoît, trans. Sheila Fischman. Montreal: Harvest House, 1975. *The Chelsea Journal* 2.2 (April/March 1976): 83-85.

Gives examples of oddities in the translations.

409. Kirley, Kevin. Rev. of *Marie Calumet*, by Rodolphe Girard, trans. Irène Currie. Montreal: Harvest House, 1976. *The Chelsea Journal* 4.1 (January/February 1978): 43-44.

Although the translation "has caught much of the freshness and flowing style of the original," there are occasional flaws of which a number of examples are given.

410. Kirley, Kevin. "Quebec Literature." Rev. of *French Canadian Prose Masters: The Nineteenth Century*, ed. and trans. Yves Brunelle. Montreal: Harvest House, 1978. *The Chelsea Journal* 6.1 (January/February 1980): 31.

Remarks on the occasional instance of poor translation in the story "The Roussis' Fire" by Faucher de Saint-Maurice.

411. Knutson, Simone. Rev. of *Angéline de Montbrun*, by Laure Conan, trans. Yves Brunelle. Toronto: University of Toronto Press, 1975. *Queen's Quarterly* 83.2 (Summer 1976): 351-352.

Praises the translation as masterful; gives examples of oddities and flaws.

412. La Bossière, Camille [R.]. "Tout seul." Rev. of *La Sagouine*, by Antonine Maillet, trans. Luis de Céspedes. Toronto: Simon & Pierre, 1979. *Canadian Literature* 91 (Winter 1981): 167-169.

Claims that the original does not pose problems for the translator, but comments on those areas where the translation does not adequately reflect the source text.

413. Lane, M. Travis. "Two Translations." Rev. of *Veiled Countries/ Lives*, by Marie-Claire Blais, trans. Michael Harris. Montreal: Véhicule Press, 1984. *Fiddlehead* 144 (Summer 1985): 100-103.

While the translations are "mostly good English poetry," the translator is criticized for shortening "Blais's lines, making them conform to the typically short-winded Anglophone Canadian pattern, rather than leaving them in the long breaths Blais gives them."

414. Laprès, Raymond. Compte rendu du *Lion avait un visage d'homme*, par Robertson Davies, trad. Claire Martin. Montréal: Éditions Pierre Tisseyre, 1978. *Nos livres (Livres canadiens)* 10 (mars 1979): 91.

Commente cette traduction "réussie et les quelques rares lourdeurs."

415. Lefrançois, Alexis. "'Accueillir le plus profond rêve du temps.'" Compte rendu des *Poèmes des quatre côtés*, par Jacques Brault. Saint-Lambert: Éditions du Noroît, 1975. *Liberté* 17.100 (juillet/ août, 1975): 57-65.

Cite et décrit les théories de Brault sur la nontraduction et le concept de "l'originalité du texte" [voir 174].

416. Legris, Maurice. Rev. of *The Journal of Saint-Denys Garneau*, trans. John Glassco. Toronto: McClelland and Stewart, 1962. *Dalhousie Review* 43.3 (Autumn 1963): 427-429.

Discusses the scarcity of translations and the idea of translation as a bridge between cultures; claims this is a good translation.

417.　Leith, Linda. Rev. of *Nights in the Underground*, by Marie-Claire Blais, trans. Ray Ellenwood. Don Mills, Ontario: Musson, 1979. *Quill & Quire* 45.8 (July 1979): 49-50.

Discusses the skill with which Ellenwood has rendered the "rough and lively dialogue," but suggests that "long and gentle passages of narration" are more important to the novel, and that his translation "lacks the beauty of Blais's original French"; mentions the nature of these "eye-catching" flaws.

418.　Leith, Linda. "Rights of Memory." Rev. of *Hamlet's Twin*, by Hubert Aquin, trans. Sheila Fischman. Toronto: McClelland and Stewart, 1979; and *Nights in the Underground*, by Marie-Claire Blais, trans. Ray Ellenwood. Don Mills, Ontario: Musson, 1979. *The Canadian Forum* 59 (September 1979): 28-29.

Comments on Fischman's background and success as a translator; questions why the original title was not translated literally as "Black Snow," although "Hamlet's Twin" has textual significance; while Ellenwood has successfully translated the dialogue in Blais's novel, "the sense of flowing movement and lyricism that one finds in Blais's French" is lacking.

419.　Leith, Linda. "A Taste of Earth." Rev. of *Bitter Bread*, by Albert Laberge, trans. Conrad Dion. Montreal: Harvest House, 1977. *Canadian Literature* 82 (Autumn 1979): 120-121.

Although claims that the tone of Laberge's French is captured by the translator, lists a few examples of translation flaws.

420.　Leney, Jane. "Seven Cuts." Rev. of *A Québécois Dream*, by Victor-Lévy Beaulieu, trans. Ray Chamberlain. Toronto: Exile Editions, 1978. *Brick: A Journal of Reviews* 9 (Spring 1980): 31-33.

Comments on the naturalness of the translation, discusses the difficulty of translating slang and communicating "the flavour of the French"; gives a few examples of Chamberlain's effective substitution of "non-standard English for non-standard French."

421.　Lennox, John. "Survivors from History." Rev. of *Pélagie*, by Antonine Maillet, trans. Philip Stratford. Toronto: Doubleday, 1982. *Essays on Canadian Writing* 28 (Spring 1984): 156-159.

Claims that the translation is "delightful and high-spirited"; Stratford has captured the colloquial flavour and conveyed the novel's style and humour.

422. L'Heureux, J.M. "Translating French-Canadian Poetry." Rev. of *The Poetry of French Canada in Translation*, ed. John Glassco. Toronto: Oxford University Press, 1970; and *One Hundred Poems of Modern Quebec*, trans. Fred Cogswell. Fredericton: Fiddlehead Poetry Books, 1970. *The Canadian Forum* 50 (July/August 1970): 182-183.

Discusses why English-Canadian poets translate French-Canadian poetry despite the technical difficulties or the criticism that translating is foolish or "faintly sacrilegious"; summarizes Glassco's discussion of translation in his introduction to *The Poetry of French Canada in Translation* [see 227]; suggests that some poems in this anthology may be untranslatable because outdated and "far from our sympathies," but claims that most of the poetry is more contemporary and thus the translations are "much richer and above all more rigorous"; refers to Scott's translation of Saint-Denys Garneau as one of the best in the text; claims that Cogswell makes the original text truly his own.

423. Lotbinière-Harwood, Susanne de. "Les Belles Infidèles." *Resources for Feminist Research/Documentation sur la recherche féministe* 14.3 (November/novembre 1985): 20.

Description de son 'Show de traduction,' "Les Belles Infidèles" [voir 81] de ses idées sur le féminisme et sur la langue dans la traduction.

424. Macri, Francis M. "A Skeleton Closet." Rev. of *The Torrent*, by Anne Hébert, trans. Gwendolyn Moore. Montreal: Harvest House, 1973. *Journal of Canadian Fiction* 3.2 (1974): 105-106.

Discusses in detail the difficulty and process of translation, and examines the problems in this rendering, which "suffers a great deal from technical and stylistic inadequacy."

425. Malden, Peter and Jean-Claude Marineau. Rev. of *Embers and Earth*, by Gaston Miron, trans. D.G. Jones and Marc Plourde. Bilingual Edition. Montreal: Guernica Editions, 1984. *Rubicon* 5 (Summer 1985): 138-142.

Summarizes and comments on Plourde's essay "On Translating Miron" [see 252]; mentions, with examples, the difficulties faced by a translator.

426.   Manguel, Alberto. "Tour of Quebec that's worth visit." Rev. of *The Alley Cat*, by Yves Beauchemin, trans. Sheila Fischman. Toronto: McClelland and Stewart, 1986. *The Ottawa Citizen* Books (Saturday, August 16, 1986): C3.

Questions whether certain forms of speech such as Beauchemin's "wittily crafted turns of phrase . . . can undergo the metamorphosis of translation and still live"; outlines the difficulties and process of literary translation; comments on the personalized speech in the novel, and claims that the problem of finding "an exact English equivalent for these ways of speech is, of course, unthinkable, and Sheila Fischman's attempt . . . is only as effective as it can be."

427.   Mantz, Douglas. Rev. of *Farewell, Babylon*, by Naïm Kattan, trans. Sheila Fischman. Toronto: McClelland and Stewart, 1976. *Canadian Fiction Magazine* 24/25 (Spring/Summer 1977): 179-181.

Claims that the translation "preserves the humour and ironic innuendoes" of the original, but that there are some oddities in the translation.

428.   Marchand, Pierre. "À propos de la traduction du Tombeau des rois." Compte rendu du *Dialogue sur la traduction à propos du Tombeau des rois*, par Anne Hébert et F.R. Scott. Montréal: Éditions HMH, 1970. *Meta* 21.2 (juin 1976): 155-160.

Réponse au compte rendu de Jean Delisle [voir 353] et analyse du *Dialogue sur la traduction* [voir 176] et de la traduction du "Tombeau des rois" d'Anne Hébert par F.R. Scott.

429.   Marcotte, Gilles. "Hugh MacLennan parmi nous: Vous n'avez peut-être pas lu 'Barometer Rising.' Lirez-vous 'Le Temps tournera au beau'?" Compte rendu du *Temps tournera au beau*, par Hugh MacLennan, trad. de Jean Simard. *La Presse* Supplément Arts et Lettres (7 mai 1966): 1-3.

Replace la traduction qu'a faite Jean Simard de *Barometer Rising* dans le contexte de la réception réservée au travail de MacLennan au niveau anglais, français et international.

430.   Marcotte, Gilles. "La Poésie." Compte rendu de *The Poetry of French Canada in Translation*, ed. John Glassco. Toronto: Oxford University Press, 1970. *Études françaises* 77.1 (février 1971): 103-114.

S'accorde avec Glassco pour reconnaître que cela représente plus une anthologie de traductions qu'une anthologie de poésie canadienne-française traduite en anglais; remet en question l'affirmation de Glassco selon laquelle la traduction est "l'épreuve la plus rigoureuse que la structure interne d'un poème puisse subir"; signale au passage un problème dans la traduction de Roland Giguère et d'Alain Grandbois; indique qu'une "poésie qui se refuserait absolument à la traduction ne serait peut-être pas autre chose qu'un vain jeu de mots."

431.   Marineau, Jean-Claude. See 425.

432.   Marshall, Joyce. "Three from the Other Nation." Rev. of *Prochain épisode*, by Hubert Aquin, trans. Penny Williams. Toronto: McClelland and Stewart, 1967. *The Tamarack Review* 46 (Winter 1968): 109-110.

Discussion of the intensity of Aquin's style and the almost inherent impossibility of translating a text which "so barely worked in French"; describes what would necessarily be involved in reconstructing this novel in English; comments on the failure of this translation to capture the original style and the consequent failure of the novel in English—"style, it would seem, was all."

433.   Mathews, Robin. Rev. of *The Agonized Life*, by Gaston Miron, trans. Marc Plourde. Montreal: Torchy Wharf Press, 1980. *The Canadian Forum* 60 (November 1980): 35.

Criticizes the flaws in the translation; claims that the intention of the original is not always expressed.

434.   McPherson, Hugo. "Blais, Godbout, Roy; Love, Art, Time." Rev. of *The Manuscripts of Pauline Archange*, by Marie-Claire Blais, trans. Derek Coltman. New York: Farrar, Straus & Giroux, 1970; *Hail Galarneau!*, by Jacques Godbout, trans. Alan Brown. Toronto: Longman Canada, 1970; and *Windflower*, by Gabrielle Roy, trans. Joyce Marshall. Toronto: McClelland and Stewart, 1970. *The Tamarack Review* 57 (Spring 1971): 85-86.

Claims that the translation of all three novels is excellent with a brief note on each explaining why. Comments in more detail on the difficulty of translating the *joual* of *Hail Galarneau!*.

435.   McPherson, Hugo. "Prodigies of God and Man." Rev. of *The Hidden Mountain*, by Gabrielle Roy, trans. Harry Lorin Binsse.

Toronto: McClelland and Stewart, 1961. *Canadian Literature* 15 (Winter 1963): 74-76.

Comments on the omission of an important sentence from the original.

436. Meadwell, Kenneth W. Compte rendu de *First Secrets and Other Poems*, by Éloi de Grandmont, trans. Daniel Sloate. Bilingual Edition. Montreal: Guernica Editions, 1983; and *Veiled Countries/ Lives*, by Marie-Claire Blais, trans. Michael Harris. Montreal: Signal Editions, 1984. *Quarry* 34.2 (Spring 1985): 78-80.

"La version anglaise est fidèle à l'original" (Grandmont), et "un succès incontestable" (Blais).

437. Merivale, Patricia. "'Appendix on the Translation,' Chiaroscuro: *Neige noire/Hamlet's Twin*." Rev. of *Hamlet's Twin*, by Hubert Aquin, trans. Sheila Fischman. Toronto: McClelland and Stewart, 1979. *Dalhousie Review* 60.2 (Summer 1980): 330-333.

While the translation is "distinctly good," there are "enough errors, misjudgements and questions of tone to blur the impact of Aquin's text for the Anglophone reader," especially the "re-translation into English of Aquin's quotations from Shakespeare," as well as the omission of an epigraph, significant reflections, puns.

438. Merivale, Patricia. "Ideologies." Rev. of *The Euguélionne*, by Louky Bersianik, trans. Gerry Dennis, Alison Hewitt, Donna Murray, and Martha O'Brien. Erin, Ontario: Press Porcépic, 1980. *Canadian Literature* 102 (Autumn 1984): 130-133.

Discusses the difficulty of translating parts of Bersianik's text because of the "peculiarities of French"; judges the translation favourably, despite "the inevitable loss or blurring of some of the jokes."

439. Merivale, Patricia. "Pot Pourri." Rev. of *The Jimmy Trilogy*, by Jacques Poulin, trans. Sheila Fischman. Toronto: Anansi, 1979; and *Contemporary Quebec Criticism*, ed. and trans. Larry Shouldice. Toronto: University of Toronto Press, 1979. *Canadian Literature* 88 (Spring 1981): 127-133.

Comments on the untranslatability of some of the puns in Poulin's book; mentions what elements of the original style are expressed in translation and lists a few examples; in regard to *Contemporary Quebec Criticism*, states that the French text should have been printed alongside the translation so that the reader could clarify ambiguous meanings in the English version.

440. Merler, Grazia. Rev. of *Héloïse*, by Anne Hébert, trans. Sheila Fischman. Toronto: Stoddart, 1983. *West Coast Review* 18.1 (June 1983): 60-64.

Discusses the skill required to translate a work such as this one and the inevitable interpretation that takes place, particularly because "perlocutionary utterances are obviously difficult to render in translation"; provides a number of examples in the translation where "parenthetical utterances" either deviate from the original or are omitted, and where change in tense fails to communicate the specific tone of the original.

441. Mezei, Kathy. Rev. of *The Antiphonary*, by Hubert Aquin, trans. Alan Brown. Toronto: Anansi, 1973. *Quarry* 22.4 (Autumn 1973): 74-75.

Praises the translation, as "this cannot have been an easy book to do."

442. Mezei, Kathy. Rev. of *Contemporary Quebec Criticism*, trans. and ed. Larry Shouldice. Toronto: University of Toronto Press, 1979. *Canadian Review of Comparative Literature/Revue canadienne de littérature comparée* 9.1 (March 1982): 133-136.

Discusses in some detail the difficulty of translating a number of these essays—"although one assumes that he would be relieved of the painful dilemmas involved in poetry and fiction, he is faced with other, equally stringent decisions"; the styles of individual essayists and critical terminology specific to French present particular problems.

443. Mezei, Kathy. "From Dragons to Deserts." Rev. of *Dragon Island*, by Jacques Godbout, trans. David Ellis. Don Mills, Ontario: Musson, 1978. *Canadian Literature* 86 (Autumn 1980): 119-121.

Discusses the difficulty of capturing the tone of the original in English; comments on the difference in narratorial tone because of change in verb tense; claims that reading the translation is "a different kind of experience."

444. Mezei, Kathy. Rev. of *The Fugitive*, by Marie-Claire Blais, trans. David Lobdell. Vancouver: Talonbooks, 1978. *Room of One's Own* 4.4 (1979): 76-78.

States that the translation is skilfully done with a few lapses, and is truer to the original than his translation of *Dürer's Angel.*

445. Mezei, Kathy. Rev. of *The Garden of Delights*, by Roch Carrier, trans. Sheila Fischman. Toronto: Anansi, 1978. *West Coast Review* 13.2 (October 1978): 54-55.

Fischman's translation has caught Carrier's tone, humour, and conciseness; she resolved the problem of *joual* by using mild slang.

446. Mezei, Kathy. Rev. of *Nights in the Underground*, by Marie-Claire Blais, trans. Ray Ellenwood. Don Mills, Ontario: Musson, 1979; and *Hamlet's Twin*, by Hubert Aquin, trans. Sheila Fischman. Toronto: McClelland and Stewart, 1979. *Queen's Quarterly* 87.1 (Spring 1980): 161-162.

Claims that Ellenwood's translation, which improves throughout the novel, gives us a more prosaic Blais; he also has difficulty translating the colloquial dialogue; some English phrases in the source text are translated into French, others are left in English. Fischman's translation is accomplished.

447. Mezei, Kathy. Rev. of *The Oxford Book of French-Canadian Short Stories*, ed. Richard Teleky, introduced by Marie-Claire Blais. Toronto: Oxford University Press, 1983. *Anglo-French Literary Relations.* Special number of *The Yearbook of English Studies* 15 (1985): 253-254.

Remarks on the unease exhibited in a few of the stories when the translator has attempted "to capture the colloquial voice and dialects, the tone of the folktale and the aura of story telling"; in general, the translations are "accurate and readable."

448. Mezei, Kathy. "Pauline Archange Revisited." Rev. of *Dürer's Angel*, by Marie-Claire Blais, trans. David Lobdell. Vancouver: Talonbooks, 1976. *Journal of Canadian Fiction* 24: 134-137.

Comments on the significance of Lobdell's title, *Dürer's Angel*, which is "more pointed than Blais's own *Les Apparences*"; discusses and gives examples of the change in tone in the translation due to the liberties taken with the source text and to differences between French and English.

449. Micros, Marianne. "Rape and Ritual." Rev. of *Children of the Black Sabbath*, by Anne Hébert, trans. Carol Dunlop-Hébert. Don Mills,

Ontario: Musson, 1977. *Essays on Canadian Writing* 7/8 (Fall 1977): 31-34.

Although very literal, the translation retains "the poetry, subtlety, and complex mood of Hébert's work."

450. Monk, Patricia. Rev. of *The Alchemy of the Body*, by Juan Garcia, trans. Marc Plourde. Fredericton: Fiddlehead Poetry Books, 1974. *Quarry* 24.4 (Autumn 1975): 61-62.

Criticizes the translation as inadequate and clumsy; speculates whether it fails due to the translator's "lack of imagination and/ or experience with the English language," or to obscurity in the original text.

451. Moorhead, Andrea. Rev. of *The Ceremony*, by Marie-José Thériault, trans. David Lobdell. Ottawa: Oberon Press, 1980. *Quarry* 30.1 (Winter 1981): 86-88.

Praises the rich and exact translation of the lyrical and descriptive passages.

452. Moritz, Albert. "Hébert with Anglo-Saxon Flair." Rev. of *Poems by Anne Hébert*, trans. Alfred Poulin, Jr. Contemporary Poetry Series. *Quarterly Review of Literature* 21.3/4 (1980). *Books in Canada* 9.9 (November 1980): 20.

Comparison of Poulin's translations of Hébert with those of Alan Brown and F.R. Scott—Poulin has found a "new tone . . . in Hébert—a more colloquial, speech-based tone than was heard by Scott and Brown"; he "achieves a voice that does not disguise the poet's own"; Brown and Scott, in contrast, convey Hébert's poetry in language that is more literary; compares the three translators' renditions of a verse.

453. Moss, Jane. "School Days." Rev. of *Thérèse and Pierrette and the Little Hanging Angel*, by Michel Tremblay, trans. Sheila Fischman. Toronto: McClelland and Stewart, 1984. *Canadian Literature* 103 (Winter 1984): 124-125.

Outlines Fischman's "admirable job" in translating *joual*; the translation has the characters speaking "the kind of colloquial language that lower-class anglophone Montrealers might have spoken in 1942."

454. Nelson, Ian C. Rev. of *The Impromptu of Outremont*, by Michel Tremblay, trans. John Van Burek. Vancouver: Talonbooks, 1981. *Canadian Book Review Annual* (1981): 195.

Discusses translation problems caused by linguistic tricks.

455. Nelson, Ian C. Rev. of *Sainte-Carmen of the Main*, by Michel Tremblay, trans. John Van Burek. Vancouver: Talonbooks, 1981. *Canadian Book Review Annual* (1981): 196.

Discusses problem of the translation of stage directions; translation is otherwise "colourfully rendered."

456. Neuman, Shirley. "Tender Vignettes." Rev. of *Children of My Heart*, by Gabrielle Roy, trans. Alan Brown. Toronto: McClelland and Stewart, 1979. *Branching Out* 6.4 (1979): 37-39.

States that Brown's translation is "faithful to Roy's style and tone," but there are occasional flaws.

457. O'Connor, John. "Echoes, Reflections." Rev. of *The Ceremony*, by Marie-José Thériault, trans. David Lobdell. Ottawa: Oberon Press, 1980; and *The Umbrella Pines*, by Gilles Archambault, trans. David Lobdell. Ottawa: Oberon Press, 1980. *Canadian Literature* 91 (Winter 1981): 128-131.

Discusses the purpose of translating and the ideal objective of good translation; criticizes Lobdell's other translations; claims that these two indicate improvement; analyzes the translations, focussing on flaws.

458. O'Donnell, Kathleen. "Tales on Tiptoe." Rev. of *Tales sur la pointe des pieds*, by Gilles Vigneault, trans. Paul Allard. Erin, Ontario: Press Porcépic, 1972. *Journal of Canadian Fiction* 1.4 (Fall 1972): 89-90.

Comments on the great proficiency required "to produce the exact nuance in translating from a modern French-Canadian text"; praises Allard's rendering as successful.

459. O'Neill-Karch, Mariel. "Deceiving Appearances." Rev. of *Dürer's Angel*, by Marie-Claire Blais, trans. David Lobdell. Vancouver: Talonbooks, 1976. *The Canadian Forum* 57 (June/July 1977): 58.

Criticizes translation: claims that Lobdell fails to capture the style and tone of the original, perhaps because he is not "sufficiently familiar with French language and culture."

460. Owen, I.M. "Bridge of Tongues." Rev. of *Farewell, Babylon*, by Naïm Kattan, trans. Sheila Fischman. Toronto: McClelland and Stewart, 1976. *Books in Canada* 5.12 (December 1976): 5-6.

Comments on the success of this translation and his own attempts to translate the "beautiful but not (to put it mildly) limpid" prose of Kattan; makes some criticism of Fischman's translation; discusses the difficulty involved in translating, the inevitable tendency for the rendering to become "progressively more literal and less English"; remarks on the need for an editor to advise the translator and suggest possible improvements.

461. Partridge, Colin. Rev. of *Is It the Sun, Philibert?*, by Roch Carrier, trans. Sheila Fischman. Toronto: Anansi, 1972. *Canadian Fiction Magazine* 10 (Spring 1973): 98-106.

Claims that Fischman's "translation captures much of the spirit of the original," but asserts that the tone and some of the word play are not captured.

462. Peterman, Michael A. "Ordered Madness." Rev. of *The Scarecrows of Saint-Emmanuel*, by André Major, trans. Sheila Fischman. Toronto: McClelland and Stewart, 1977; and *Don Quixote in Nighttown*, by Victor-Lévy Beaulieu, trans. Sheila Fischman. Erin, Ontario: Press Porcépic, 1978. *Canadian Literature* 99 (Spring 1981): 100-104.

Comments on the skill of Fischman's translations; makes specific reference to the difficulty of translating Beaulieu because of the "many areas of perplexity" created by his style.

463. Raspa, Anthony [N.]. "Les Chambres de bois." Rev. of *The Silent Rooms*, by Anne Hébert, trans. Kathy Mezei. Don Mills, Ontario: Musson, 1974. *Journal of Canadian Fiction* 15 (1976): 173-175.

Outlines the development of the translation from a too literal to a more symbolic and image-conscious rendering of Hébert's prose; provides some examples of translation problems.

464. Raspa, Anthony [N.]. "Epic Blais in Translation." Rev. of *St. Lawrence Blues*, by Marie-Claire Blais, trans. Ralph Manheim. New York: Bantam Books, 1976. *Journal of Canadian Fiction* 19 (1977): 138-140.

Short but substantial discussion of the difficulty of translating *joual* and Québécois swear words.

465. Raspa, Anthony N. Rev. of *White Niggers of America*, by Pierre Vallières, trans. Joan Pinkham. New York: Monthly Review Press, 1971. *Dalhousie Review* 51 (Summer 1971): 292-293, 295.

Claims that Pinkham "is faithful to the aphorisms of Vallières' style" in the earlier boyhood parts, because "the prose . . . [is] more poetic, its phrasing . . . looser and easier to render into English" than later "shrill sections describing Vallières' public life in journalism"; the maintenance of French cadences in the translation renders part of the text confusing.

466. Rekai, Julie. Rev. of *The Death of André Breton*, by Jean Yves Collette, trans. Ray Chamberlain. Montreal: Guernica Editions, 1984. *Canadian Book Review Annual* (1984): 181-182.

Points out the differences in nuances between French and English, and claims that the translation fails because it is too literal.

467. Rekai, Julie. Rev. of *La Sagouine*, by Antonine Maillet, trans. Luis de Céspedes. Toronto: Simon & Pierre, 1979. *Canadian Book Review Annual* (1982): 218.

"The excellent translation from the Acadian 'argot' to English dialect retains every subtle nuance of the original text."

468. Rekai, Julie. Rev. of *Veiled Countries/Lives*, by Marie-Claire Blais, trans. Michael Harris. Montreal: Signal Editions, 1984. *Canadian Book Review Annual* (1984): 215.

Praises the skill with which the translator "carefully sustains all the nuances and subtleties of each poem."

469. Ricard, François. "Littérature québécoise: livres de poésie." Compte rendu des *Poèmes des quatre côtés*, par Jacques Brault. Saint-Lambert: Éditions du Noroît, 1975. *Liberté* 17.14 (juillet/août 1975): 100-111.

Présente la disposition structurelle des *Poèmes des quatre côtés*, l'importance des titres et des passages en prose; décrit la façon dont ces passages en prose sont, en fait, une réflexion sur le fait de créer des traductions poétiques et la manière dont le lecteur participe à la création de ces dernières; analyse en détail le concept de Brault sur la nontraduction, concept complexe et paradoxal car il "signifie rapprochement et distance, fusion et rupture . . . la liberté" [voir 174].

470. Rièse, Laure. "Christian Poetry in Translation." Rev. of *St.-Denys Garneau and Anne Hébert*, trans. F.R. Scott. Vancouver: Klanak Press, 1962. *The Canadian Forum* 42 (December 1962): 210.

Brief commentary emphasizing Scott's sensitivity as a translator.

471. Rièse, Laure. Rev. of *Twelve Modern French Canadian Poets*, trans. G.R. Roy. Bilingual Edition. Toronto: The Ryerson Press, 1958. *The Canadian Forum* 38 (March 1959): 286.

Discusses the difficulty of translation, the problem of too literal translation, and the role of a translator.

472. Ripley, John. "Two Bondage Plays: Sparks Not Incandescence." Rev. of *The Fairies Are Thirsty*, by Denise Boucher, trans. Alan Brown. Vancouver: Talonbooks, 1982. *Essays on Canadian Writing* 30 (Winter 1984/85): 304-307.

Calls the translation a "cultural transposition"; lists a few examples of Brown's discovery of English equivalents for certain untranslatable terms, as well as some examples of inadequate translation.

473. Roberts-Van Oordt, Christina H. Rev. of *Kamouraska*, by Anne Hébert, trans. Norman Shapiro. Don Mills, Ontario: Musson, 1973. *The Canadian Forum* 53 (November/December 1973): 32-33.

Claims that Hébert's "highly complex style of imagery" could not be entirely conveyed in translation, and that Shapiro's rendering "moves along smoothly and doesn't stand in the way of the original too much."

474. Roberts-Van Oordt, Christina H. Rev. of *The Wolf*, by Marie-Claire Blais, trans. Sheila Fischman. Toronto: McClelland and Stewart, 1974; and *They Won't Demolish Me!*, by Roch Carrier, trans. Sheila Fischman. Toronto: Anansi, 1974. *Queen's Quarterly* 82.2 (Summer 1975): 294-295.

Claims that both translations are basically excellent; gives examples of a number of translation flaws in *The Wolf* that could have been prevented if the text had been checked by a competent translation editor.

475. Rudzik, O.H.T. Rev. of *The Wolf*, by Marie-Claire Blais, trans. Sheila Fischman. Toronto: McClelland and Stewart, 1974. *The University of Toronto Quarterly* 44.4 (Summer 1975): 311.

Since the "metaphysics of passion and personality are a risky undertaking into a translated context that avoids any such novelistic tradition," the translation "has lost its intended ferocity."

476. Russell, D.W. Rev. of *Garden in the Wind*, by Gabrielle Roy, trans. Alan Brown. Toronto: McClelland and Stewart, 1977; and *Children*

of My Heart, by Gabrielle Roy, trans. Alan Brown. Toronto: McClelland and Stewart, 1979. *Fiddlehead* 122 (Summer 1979): 143-144.

Claims that the translations are "nearly faultless"; gives one example of an "infelicitous" translation.

477. Russell, D.W. "Recent Canadian Writing." Rev. of *The Agonized Life*, by Gaston Miron, trans. and ed. Marc Plourde. Montreal: Torchy Wharf Press, 1980; *Treatise on White and Tincture*, by Robert Marteau, trans. Barry Callaghan. Toronto: Exile Editions, 1980; and *Atlante*, by Robert Marteau, trans. Barry Callaghan. Toronto: Exile Editions, 1979. *Queen's Quarterly* 89.1 (Spring 1982): 217-219.

Comments on the closeness of Plourde's translation to the original, while Callaghan "more frequently takes poetic licence with the widely allusive verse of Marteau, for understandable reasons"; includes a couple of examples of mistranslations.

478. Russell, D.W. "Le Vertige." Rev. of *Anna's World*, by Marie-Claire Blais, trans. Sheila Fischman. Toronto: Lester & Orpen Dennys, 1985. *Canadian Literature* 107 (Winter 1985): 137-139.

Comments on the quality of Fischman's translation, which "catches the tone of the original"; mentions the appearance of some obtrusive phrases.

479. Ryder, Carolyn. Rev. of *Fear's Folly*, by Jean-Charles Harvey, trans. John Glassco. Ottawa: Carleton University Press, 1982. *Canadian Book Review Annual* (1982): 144-145.

Comments on the excellent quality of the translation.

480. Saint-Pierre, Annette. Compte rendu de *Canada's Lost Plays, Volume Four, Colonial Quebec: French-Canadian Drama, 1606-1966*, ed. Anton Wagner. Toronto: Canadian Theatre Review Publications, 1982. *Theatre History in Canada/Histoire du théâtre au Canada* 4.2 (Fall 1983): 211-212.

Fait l'éloge des traducteurs et commente l'importance de traduire ces textes et de les rendre facilement accessibles pour le public anglophone.

481. Salesse, Michelle. "L'Homme invisible/The Invisible Man." Compte rendu de *L'Homme invisible/The Invisible Man: un récit/A Story*, par/by Patrice Desbiens. Sudbury, Ontario: Éditions Prise de Parole/

Moonbeam, Ontario: Penumbra Press, 1981. *Lettres québécoises* 26 (été 1982): 79-80.

Se demande s'il s'agit réellement d'une traduction; compare deux versions du texte à l'aide d'exemples.

482.   Scott, Chris. "Well Made in Orleans." Rev. of *The Madman, the Kite and the Island*, by Félix Leclerc, trans. Philip Stratford. Ottawa: Oberon Press, 1976. *Books in Canada* 5.12 (December 1976): 24.

Comments on the quality of the translation, which renders "the lyric cadences of the original."

483.   Seed, Deborah. "Murder in Joual." Rev. of *The Scarecrows of Saint-Emmanuel*, by André Major, trans. Sheila Fischman. Toronto: McClelland and Stewart, 1977. *Matrix* 3.6/7 (1978): 131-133.

Praises Fischman as having "reproduced the author's poetic diction and the rhythm of his prose with sensitivity"; comments on her skilful translation of *joual*.

484.   Shek, Ben-Zion. "A Separatist Novel Written in a Quebec Jail." Rev. of *Prochain épisode*, by Hubert Aquin, trans. Penny Williams. Toronto: McClelland and Stewart, 1967. *The Toronto Star* (Saturday 6 May 1967): 78.

Outlines the translation flaws: the problems of too literal translation, mistranslation, omission, and the banal rendering of Aquin's poetic, erotic language.

485.   Shohet, Linda. Rev. of *Dr. Cotnoir*, by Jacques Ferron, trans. Pierre Cloutier. Montreal: Harvest House, 1973. *Canadian Fiction Magazine* 16 (Winter 1975): 101-104.

Claims that the translation is well done, and discusses why Ferron is tricky to translate; includes some reference to and examples from *Tales from the Uncertain Country*, trans. Betty Bednarski.

486.   Shohet, Linda. Rev. of *The Torrent*, by Anne Hébert, trans. Gwendolyn Moore. Montreal: Harvest House, 1973. *Canadian Fiction Magazine* 15 (Autumn 1974): 97-99.

Discusses the Hébert-Scott dialogue on translation [see 176]; criticizes the translation of *The Torrent* as too literal, often awkward, and failing to capture the spirit of the original.

487. Shouldice, Larry. "Anne Hébert Translated." Rev. of *Poems by Anne Hébert*, trans. Alan Brown. Don Mills, Ontario: Musson, 1975. *Matrix* 2.1 (Spring 1976): 22-23.

Begins with a lengthy discussion of translation in Canada—the increase in the number of translations as well as the improved quality; mentions other translations of Hébert's poetry, praising Brown's translations as best capturing the tone and style of the originals; refers to *Dialogue sur la traduction* and comments made by Northrop Frye in his introduction [see 176; 221].

488. Shouldice, Larry. Rev. of *Histoire de la traduction au Canada*. Numéro spécial de *Meta* 22.1 (mars 1977). *Canadian Review of Comparative Literature/Revue canadienne de littérature comparée* 7.4 (Fall 1980): 476-478.

Summarizes the various approaches to and theories of translation presented by the journal's contributors.

489. Sirois, Antoine. Compte rendu de *Bibliography of Canadian Books in Translation: French to English and English to French/Bibliographie de livres canadiens traduits de l'anglais au français et du français à l'anglais*, by/par Philip Stratford and/et Maureen Newman. Prepared for the Committee on Translation of the Humanities Research Council of Canada/préparé pour le Comité de la traduction du Conseil canadien de recherches sur les humanités. Ottawa: Humanities Research Council of Canada/Conseil canadien de recherches sur les humanités, 1975. *Canadian Review of Comparative Literature/Revue canadienne de littérature comparée* 3.3 (Fall 1976): 320-321.

Décrit la teneur de la bibliographie et assure qu'il faut continuer à produire des bibliographies et des traductions.

490. Skelton, Robin. "Canadian Poetry?" Rev. of "The Tomb of Kings," by Anne Hébert, trans. F.R. Scott. *The Tamarack Review* 29 (August 1963): 71-82.

Comparison of the original with the translation, which is less musical.

491. Smart, Patricia. Rev. of *The Antiphonary*, by Hubert Aquin, trans. Alan Brown. Toronto: Anansi, 1973. *Queen's Quarterly* 81.2 (Summer 1974): 313-314.

Comments on how Brown's translation fails to render the " 'fragmentalist' style of the original."

492. Smith, Beverley. "Ordinary Odd Folk." Rev. of *Tales from the Uncertain Country*, by Jacques Ferron, trans. Betty Bednarski. Toronto: Anansi, 1972. *Books in Canada* 1.9 (June 1972): 9-10.

States that Ferron's writing is enhanced by translation; praises Bednarski's rendering because it "has successfully preserved both the flavour and the rhythms of Ferron's speech."

493. Socken, Paul. Rev. of *Les Belles Sœurs*, by Michel Tremblay, trans. John Van Burek and Bill Glassco. Vancouver: Talonbooks, 1974; and *Forever Yours, Marie-Lou*, by Michel Tremblay, trans. John Van Burek and Bill Glassco. Vancouver: Talonbooks, 1975. *Queen's Quarterly* 86.2 (Summer 1979): 365-366.

Discusses how *Les Belles Sœurs* would be more successful if "adapted rather than merely translated," and claims that "much of the mood and texture of the original is lost"; gives numerous examples of mistranslations, linguistic inaccuracies, "unwarranted additions," changes and omissions; *Forever Yours, Marie-Lou* has less frequent ' lapses and is "on the whole, more linguistically accurate" than *Les Belles Sœurs*.

494. Socken, Paul. "Hollow Men." Rev. of *The Scarecrows of Saint-Emmanuel*, by André Major, trans. Sheila Fischman. Toronto: McClelland and Stewart, 1977. *The Canadian Forum* 58 (May 1978): 40.

Comments on the conveyance of a "delicate but important nuance" in the translation of the title.

495. Spencer, Nigel. "Plays from Quebec." Rev. of *Forever Yours, Marie-Lou*, by Michel Tremblay, trans. John Van Burek and Bill Glassco. Vancouver: Talonbooks, 1975; *Les Belles Sœurs*, by Michel Tremblay, trans. John Van Burek and Bill Glassco. Vancouver: Talonbooks, 1974; *Hosanna*, by Michel Tremblay, trans. John Van Burek and Bill Glassco. Vancouver: Talonbooks, 1974; *API 2967*, by Robert Gurik, trans. Mark F. Gélinas. Vancouver: Talonbooks, 1974; and *The Trial of Jean-Baptiste M.*, by Robert Gurik, trans. Allan Van Meer. Vancouver: Talonbooks, 1974. *Matrix* 1.1 (Spring 1975): 28-29.

Discussion of drama in Quebec and the untranslatability of much of the language; some reference to the translations of Guy Dufresne's *The Cry of the Whippoorwill* and Marcel Dubé's *The White Geese*; comments on each of the translations listed, and on those aspects of the plays' original tone and style that are lost in translation; concludes with the suggestion that some plays, which cannot be adequately translated, should be adapted within an anglophone context.

496. Spettigue, D.O. Rev. of *Farewell, Babylon*, by Naïm Kattan, trans. Sheila Fischman. Toronto: McClelland and Stewart, 1976. *Queen's Quarterly* 84.3 (Autumn 1977): 510-511.

Comments on the difficulty of translating the nuances of a culture and "language two and three times removed from us."

497. Stratford, Philip. "Anne Hébert's Romance of Evil." Rev. of *Children of the Black Sabbath*, by Anne Hébert, trans. Carol Dunlop-Hébert. Don Mills, Ontario: Musson, 1977. *Quill & Quire* 43.5 (April 1977): 38.

Remarks on the quality of the translations of all her books, and then on *Children of the Black Sabbath*, which "catches the nervous power and demonic hilarity of the original" but "lacks the inevitability of great translation."

498. Stratford, Philip. "Circle, Straight Line, Ellipse." Rev. of *The Poetry of French Canada in Translation*, ed. John Glassco. Toronto: Oxford University Press, 1970; and *One Hundred Poems of Modern Quebec*, ed. Fred Cogswell. Fredericton: Fiddlehead Poetry Books, 1970. *Canadian Literature* 49 (Summer 1971): 88-91.

Comments on translation in Canada and on the accomplishment represented by these works; discusses and compares the quality of the translations in both books, with some examples, and reflects on the art of translating; compares the translation of two of the poems in Cogswell's collection with F.R. Scott's translation of the same and explains why, in these instances, he prefers Cogswell's renderings.

499. Stratford, Philip. "Existential Vertigo." Rev. of *Wings in the Wind*, by Diane Giguère, trans. Alan Brown. Toronto: McClelland and Stewart, 1979. *Essays on Canadian Writing* 16 (Fall/Winter 1979/80): 213-218.

Criticizes the translation as complacent, although the text is deemed difficult "to translate for obvious reasons."

500. Stratford, Philip. Rev. of *The Fat Woman Next Door Is Pregnant*, by Michel Tremblay, trans. Sheila Fischman. Vancouver: Talon-books, 1981. *Quill & Quire* 48.2 (February 1982): 38.

Notes that Fischman's rendering does not read at all like a translation.

501. Stratford, Philip. "Marie-Claire Blais: Prowling the Periphery of Solitude." Rev. of *Deaf to the City*, by Marie-Claire Blais, trans. Carol Dunlop. Toronto: Lester & Orpen Dennys, 1981. *Quill & Quire* 47.6 (June 1981): 34.

Discusses the process and difficulty of translation, and comments on Dunlop's translation as loyal, if perhaps "a trifle more colourful than the original."

502. Stratford, Philip. "New Fiction Spans Cultural Gap." Rev. of *The Fugitive*, by Marie-Claire Blais, trans. David Lobdell. Ottawa: Oberon Press, 1978; *Dragon Island*, by Jacques Godbout, trans. David Ellis. Don Mills, Ontario: Musson, 1978; and *The Tale of Don l'Orignal*, by Antonine Maillet, trans. Barbara Godard. Toronto: Clarke Irwin, 1978. *Quill & Quire* 44.17 (December 1978): 32.

Comments on the need for more translation in Canada and on the role translation plays as a "bridge over the cultural gap"; briefly discusses Lobdell's translation of *The Fugitive* as too smooth at times; states that David Ellis's translation of *Dragon Island* captures the "truculent talk and sardonic humour" of the narrator; comments on the difficulty of translating the particular dialect in Maillet's novel, and on Godard's "heroic attempt" to convey this.

503. Stratford, Philip. Rev. of *Poems of French Canada*, trans. Frank Scott. Burnaby, B.C.: Blackfish Press, 1977. *Quill & Quire* 42.8 (June 1977): 42.

Discusses Scott's comments on his translation and his dialogue with Anne Hébert [see 258; 176].

504. Stratford, Philip. "Sparrows and Eagles." Rev. of *The Alchemy of the Body and Other Poems*, by Juan Garcia, trans. Marc Plourde. Bilingual Edition. Montreal: Guernica Editions, 1983; and *Concrete City*, by Claude Beausoleil, trans. Ray Chamberlain. Bilingual Edition. Montreal: Guernica Editions, 1983. *Canadian Literature* 102 (Autumn 1984): 159-160.

Analyzes, with examples, the problems with Plourde's too literal translation of Garcia's poetry; comments favourably on Chamberlain's translation, and gives a couple of comparative examples.

505. Stuart, Mary Alice. "Le Temps des jeux." Rev. of *Innocence*, by Diane Giguère, trans. Peter Green. Toronto: McClelland and Stewart, 1962. *The Canadian Forum* 41 (December 1962): 206-207.

Claims that the translation is awkward and "insensitive . . . one is astonished, from the title on, at what Miss Giguère has apparently permitted in the translation"; questions why the title is not a direct translation of the original title, which "chose to emphasize *Le Temps des jeux.*"

506. Sullivan, Rosemary. "World of Two Faces." Rev. of *The Wolf*, by Marie-Claire Blais, trans. Sheila Fischman. Toronto: McClelland and Stewart, 1974. *Canadian Literature* 63 (Winter 1975): 120-122.

Discusses specific problems in translating from French to English, and how Fischman's translation succeeds.

507. Sutherland, Fraser. "Tempest in a Stewpot." Rev. of *Fear's Folly*, by Jean-Charles Harvey, trans. John Glassco. Ottawa: Carleton University Press, 1982. *Books in Canada* 12.5 (May 1983): 14.

Comments on Glassco as the "right man to prepare a new translation" [see 249].

508. Tacium, David. Rev. of *Veiled Countries/Lives*, by Marie-Claire Blais, trans. Michael Harris. Montreal: Véhicule Press, 1984. *Rubicon* 5 (Summer 1985): 176-178.

Criticizes the translator's reversification of the poetry, and claims that the translation "tries to strap the original with a degree of artifice for which there is no textual support."

509. Talbot, Émile J. Rev. of *Dialogue sur la traduction à propos du "Tombeau des rois,"* by Anne Hébert and Frank Scott. Montréal: Éditions HMH, 1970. *French Review* 45.1 (October 1971): 243-244.

Summarizes and discusses the form and content of the dialogue; lists and comments on a number of examples of the translation changes made by Scott after his consultation with Hébert; mentions the responses of Hébert and Scott to the process of their discussion and the translation [see 176].

510. Tierney, Bill. Rev. of *La Guerre, Yes Sir!*, by Roch Carrier, trans. Sheila Fischman. Toronto: Anansi, 1970. *Antigonish Review* 2.1 (Spring 1971): 89-90.

Claims that the novel is cleverly translated, and that Fischman has conveyed the "Quebec argot, all those swear-words built round religious objects and figures."

511. Tougas, Gérard. Rev. of *St.-Denys Garneau and Anne Hébert*, trans. F.R. Scott. Vancouver: Klanak Press, 1962. *Queen's Quarterly* 70.4 (Winter 1963): 449-450.

Discussion of the translation of poetry in general and of Scott's approach to the works of Garneau and Hébert, which involves interpretation: "the faithful reproduction of the original melody on a slightly different register"; provides substantial comparative examples of the originals and translations.

512. Tougas, Gérard. "Something or Nothing." Rev. of *L'Incubation*, by Gérard Bessette, trans. Glen Shortliffe. Toronto: Macmillan, 1967. *Canadian Literature* 36 (Spring 1968): 62-67.

Praises translation; discusses difficulty of translating the style and language.

513. Trottier, Barbara. "Une anthologie en langue anglaise de la nouvelle au Canada français." Compte rendu de *The Oxford Book of French-Canadian Short Stories*. Ed. Richard Teleky. Toronto: Oxford University Press, 1983. *Écrits du Canada français* 53 (1984): 209-212.

Constate que les textes dans cette collection ont pour la plupart été bien servis par leurs traducteurs. Styles, subtilités et rythmes sont fidèlement rendus. "À part quelques maladresses . . . , on oublie qu'on est en train de lire une traduction, tellement l'anglais épouse les formes et les pensées des textes français."

514. Urbas, Jeannette. "Between Two Worlds." Rev. of *Master of the River*, by Félix-Antoine Savard, trans. Richard Howard. Montreal: Harvest House, 1976; and *The Brawl*, by Gérard Bessette, trans. Marc Lebel and Ronald Sutherland. Montreal: Harvest House, 1975. *The Canadian Forum* 57 (November 1977): 39-40.

Discusses the difficulty of translating poetic prose, "the oral and rhythmic value of the words for which there is no real equivalent in English" in Savard's novel. Comments on the untranslatability of slang and the subsequent loss of flavour in *The Brawl*.

515. Urbas, Jeannette. "Chansonnier." Rev. of *The Madman, the Kite and the Island*, by Félix Leclerc, trans. Philip Stratford. Ottawa: Oberon Press, 1976. *Essays on Canadian Writing* 7/8 (Fall 1977): 36-39.

Remarks on the inevitable loss "in the translation of any poetic text from one language to another," but claims that Stratford has successfully reproduced Félix Leclerc's work.

516. Urbas, Jeannette. "From Quebec: Something Old, Something New." Rev. of *Jean Rivard*, by Antoine Gérin-Lajoie, trans. Vida Bruce. Toronto: McClelland and Stewart, 1977; and *Between Crows and Indians*, by Roger Magini, trans. Marc Plourde. Toronto: Coach House Press, 1972. *Journal of Canadian Fiction* 22 (1978): 138-141.

Comments on both translations favourably; mentions that Magini's novel presents more stylistic problems for the translator.

517. Usmiani, Renate. Rev. of *Canada's Lost Plays, Volume 4, Colonial Quebec: French Canadian Drama 1606-1966*, ed. Anton Wagner. Toronto: Canadian Theatre Review Publications, 1982. *Canadian Drama/L'Art dramatique canadien* 9.2 (1983): 526-529.

Claims that the book will not be of great "interest to literary critics for the obvious reason that works in translation necessarily present a text which differs from the original in many crucial aspects"; refers to *Le Jeune Latour* (by Antoine Gérin-Lajoie), *The French Republicans* or *An Evening at the Tavern* (by Joseph Quesnel).

518. Usmiani, Renate. Rev. of *La Duchesse de Langeais and Other Plays*, by Michel Tremblay, trans. John Van Burek. Vancouver: Talonbooks, 1976. *Canadian Book Review Annual* (1976): 219-220.

Claims that the translations are adequate, but fail to capture Tremblay's vibrant *joual*; questions the inclusion of a number of French expressions.

519. Usmiani, Renate. Rev. of *Surrealism and Quebec Literature: History of a Cultural Revolution*, by André G. Bourassa, trans. Mark Czarnecki. Toronto: University of Toronto Press, 1984. *Canadian Book Review Annual* (1984): 296-297.

Comments on the difficulty of translation; emphasizes the value of the Translator's Note in the text [see 577].

520. Vintcent, Brian. "From Quebec, With Two Stars." Rev. of *Jos Carbone*, by Jacques Benoît, trans. Sheila Fischman. Montreal: Harvest House, 1975; and *The Juneberry Tree*, by Jacques Ferron,

trans. Ray Chamberlain. Montreal: Harvest House, 1975. *Books in Canada* 4.10 (October 1975): 21.

Mentions the French Writers of Canada series translations published by Harvest House; comments on the quality of these two translations as more professional than previous titles.

521. Vintcent, Brian. "Hébert in Awkward English." Rev. of *The Torrent*, by Anne Hébert, trans. Gwendolyn Moore. Montreal: Harvest House, 1973. *Saturday Night* 89.2 (February 1974): 34-35.

Comments on the awkwardness of the translation, which is faithful, but too literal; the "ghost of the French syntax lurks behind all her sentences."

522. Vintcent, Brian. "The Innocent Guerrillas of Roch Carrier." Rev. of *They Won't Demolish Me!*, by Roch Carrier, trans. Sheila Fischman. Toronto: Anansi, 1974. *Saturday Night* 89.8 (August 1974): 31.

Comments on the skill of Fischman's translation and includes her "as one of the very few translators of French-Canadian literature in whom one can have entire confidence"; names Philip Stratford, Alan Brown, and John Glassco in this category.

523. Vintcent, Brian. "Savouring Langevin's Tragic Vision." Rev. of *Orphan Street*, by André Langevin, trans. Alan Brown. Toronto: McClelland and Stewart, 1976. *Quill & Quire* 42.15 (November 1976): 33.

Comments that the translation is rich, but that the book is not difficult to translate; briefly describes translation in Canada and the inadequate number of books translated.

524. Vintcent, Brian. Rev. of *They Won't Demolish Me!*, by Roch Carrier, trans. Sheila Fischman. Toronto: Anansi, 1974. *Quill & Quire* 40.6 (June 1974): 12.

Claims that Fischman is one of Canada's first-rate translators; she here conveys the original with "energy and zest," remaining true to the letter and spirit of Carrier's text.

525. Vintcent, Brian. "Victimized by her obsessions." Rev. of *The Antiphonary*, by Hubert Aquin, trans. Alan Brown. Toronto: Anansi, 1973. *Saturday Night* 88.9 (September 1973): 41.

Claims that this translation is superior to that of *Prochain épisode*; comments on the skill with which Brown has rendered the "subtle growth of obsession and psychic tension."

526. Voldeng, Evelyne. "The Elusive Source Text." Rev. of *These Our Mothers Or: The Disintegrating Chapter*, by Nicole Brossard, trans. Barbara Godard. Toronto: Coach House Press, 1983. *Canadian Literature* 105 (Summer 1985): 138-139.

Discusses the difficulty of translating Brossard's writing and of Godard's choice of literal translation; although Voldeng recognizes the formidable undertaking involved in the translation, she discusses the problems that arise from Godard's interpretation of context and the difficulty of translating word play.

527. Waddington, Miriam. "Chacun sa Blais." Rev. of *St. Lawrence Blues*, by Marie-Claire Blais, trans. Ralph Manheim. New York: Farrar, Straus & Giroux, 1974; and *The Wolf*, by Marie-Claire Blais, trans. Sheila Fischman. Toronto: McClelland and Stewart, 1974. *Books in Canada* 3.7 (November 1974): 3-5.

States that "the remarkable thing about these two novels is that no one would ever guess—from reading them in translation—that both were written by the same writer," and attributes this to the different approaches of the translators and "their understanding of the symbolic and connotative nature of language"; claims that *St. Lawrence Blues* works in translation, but criticizes *The Wolf*; suggests that "cultural attitudes are not really translatable" and that the narrator thus "lacks all credibility" for the anglophone reader.

528. Walker, David. "Exorcising Demons." Rev. of *Poems by Anne Hébert*, trans. Alan Brown. Don Mills, Ontario: Musson, 1975. *The Canadian Forum* 56 (August 1976): 38-39.

States that "Brown's translation of *Poèmes* is a model of the art. The translator knows that direct translation is often the simplest and best solution"; some comparison, with examples, of Brown's translations with those by Frank Scott—the former's renderings "seem less ornamentally poetic" and are freer, while Scott "is content to translate literally."

529. Walker, Micheline. "Poetic Distinction." Rev. of *The Complete Poems of Saint-Denys Garneau*, trans. John Glassco. Ottawa: Oberon Press, 1975. *The Canadian Forum* 56 (August 1976): 39-40.

Discusses translation and Glassco's success in detail; quotes from Glassco's introduction that his translations are "faithful but not literal" [see 226]; praises the translations as "pure delight," and demonstrates, with numerous examples, how they offer "interpretation of Saint-Denys Garneau's prosody and feelings" while at the same time achieving "autonomous poetic distinction."

530. Warwick, Jack. "Poetry and Painting." Rev. of *Surrealism and Quebec Literature: History of a Cultural Revolution*, by André G. Bourassa, trans. Mark Czarnecki. Toronto: University of Toronto Press, 1984. *Canadian Literature* 105 (Summer 1985): 146-148.

Claims that the translation is good, but that the subtle translation of word play may be missed by the reader. Some criticism of the inadequate rendering of details.

531. Warwick, Jack. "Translating Brilliance." Rev. of *In an Iron Glove*, by Claire Martin, trans. Philip Stratford. Toronto: The Ryerson Press, 1968. *Canadian Literature* 42 (Autumn 1969): 82-84.

Comments on the skill of Stratford's translation, which has captured the tone and spirit of the original, and on the difficulty of translating "an author whose brio is so intimately bound to the syntax and idiom of her own language"; points out the inability of any translation to fully express all the nuances of the source text.

532. Warwick, Jack. "Vécrire." Rev. of *Hail Galarneau!*, by Jacques Godbout, trans. Alan Brown. Toronto: Longman Canada, 1970. *Canadian Literature* 49 (Summer 1971): 87-88.

Comments on the difficulty of translating this novel, and praises Brown's success in capturing much of the humour of the original; gives examples of untranslatable words in the French text.

533. Welch, Liliane. "Open to Experience." Rev. of *The Complete Poems of Émile Nelligan*, ed. and trans. Fred Cogswell. Montreal: Harvest House, 1983. *Fiddlehead* 143 (Spring 1985): 97-98.

Suggests that "only poets who feel at home in their own tongue should try their hand" at the art of translation; discusses Cogswell's approach, claiming that the volume is "a success because there is nothing artificial, unnatural or contrived about the poems in their new English version"; the translator has paid attention "above all to the texture of the words and the general movement"; emphasizes the relevance of Cogswell's art as a poet to his skill as a translator.

534. Wertheimer, Leonard. Rev. of *Wild Roses*, by Jacques Ferron, trans. Betty Bednarski. Toronto: McClelland and Stewart, 1976. *Canadian Book Review Annual* (1976): 138-139.

The translation is precise and sensitive; gives an example of the only flaw.

535. Williamson, Michael. Rev. of *One for the Road*, by Gilles Archambault, trans. David Lobdell. Ottawa: Oberon Press, 1982. *Canadian Book Review Annual* (1984): 175.

Claims that although the book is well translated, it fails to convey the musicality of the original.

536. Wilson, Milton. Rev. of *Selected Poems of Émile Nelligan*, trans. P. F. Widdows. Toronto: The Ryerson Press, 1960. *The University of Toronto Quarterly* 30.4 (July 1961): 400-401.

Claims that the translations "stick pretty closely to Nelligan's own verse-forms," but are not entirely true to the intent and tone of the originals.

537. Woodcock, George. "Gabrielle Roy as Cultural Mediator." Rev. of *Garden in the Wind*, by Gabrielle Roy, trans. Alan Brown. Toronto: McClelland and Stewart, 1977. *Saturday Night* 92.9 (November 1977): 69-72.

Comments on the swiftness with which Roy's books are translated, the popularity of her writing in English Canada, and the quality of some of the translations; claims that Brown's rendering is not "as sensitively nuanced as the Binsse translations of early Roy books"; offers brief explanations and examples.

538. Woodcock, George. "Gabrielle Roy at the Height of Her Form." Rev. of *Children of My Heart*, by Gabrielle Roy, trans. Alan Brown. Toronto: McClelland and Stewart, 1979. *Saturday Night* 94.4 (May 1979): 50-52.

Comments on the skill and sensitivity of Brown's rendering of Roy's lyrical prose.

539. Woodcock, George. "Into English." Rev. of *Selected Poems of Émile Nelligan*, trans. P.F. Widdows. Toronto: The Ryerson Press, 1960. *Canadian Literature* 13 (Summer 1962): 85.

Comments on the failure of the translation to convey Nelligan's style.

540. Allard, Paul. "Traduction en anglais des *Contes sur la pointe des pieds* de Gilles Vigneault." M.A. Université de Sherbrooke, 1969.

Introduction describes Gilles Vigneault's life and the nature of the tales, and outlines Allard's practice in translating Vigneault's poetic prose, pointing out certain problems concerning equivalences, "French Canadianisms," and dialogue.

541. Beauchesne, Rosaire. "'Félicitations, docteur!,' traduction de *Sawbones Memorial* de Sinclair Ross." M.A. Université de Sherbrooke, 1982.

Describes content and form of the novel; no discussion of translation practice or theory.

542. Bednarski, Betty. *Lire une littérature*. Thèse de doctorat (Ph.D. soutenu sur publication). Université Laval, 1986.

Thèse de 135 pages accompagnant et complétant un *Dossier de publications* (1972-1986) constitué à la fois de traductions littéraires et de textes critiques portant sur divers aspects de la littérature québécoise. La thèse elle-même examine les rapports entre traduction et lecture critique et entreprend, à partir d'un problème précis de traduction (la présence de mots anglais dans un texte québécois), une réflexion sur l'œuvre de Jacques Ferron et sur son interaction avec l'altérité anglaise.

543. Bednarski, Elizabeth [Betty]. "*Le Pays incertain* de Jacques Ferron: étude et traduction." M.A. Dalhousie University, 1970.

Conclut avec des notes détaillées sur la traduction.

544. Bégin, Alfred F. "Évaluation linguistique et stylistique des archaïsmes dans la traduction de *La Sagouine*." M.A. Université du Nouveau-Brunswick, 1980.

Compare la traduction donnée par Luis de Céspedes des "survivances rabelaisiennes" de *La Sagouine* aux traductions anglaises du xviie siècle des textes de Rabelais et souligne les problèmes qu'affrontent les traducteurs d'archaïsmes.

545. Boily, Colette. "Marcel Dubé: étude et traduction." M.A. Dalhousie University, 1980.

Traduction de *De l'autre côté du mur*; le chapitre IV, "Étude et traduction," traite des problèmes linguistiques et de ceux posés par la traduction de pièces et de dialogues.

546. Brierley, Jane. "An English translation of the first edition of the *Mémoires* (1866) of Philippe-Joseph Aubert de Gaspé, with biographical and historical annotations." M.A. McGill University, 1982.

Introduction consists of biographical and historical information and a literary appreciation of the *Mémoires*; brief description of translation choices and practice.

547. Cox, Barbara. "Une traduction de six nouvelles québécoises des années 60." M.A. Université de Sherbrooke, 1985.

Translation of six short stories published in *Châtelaine*, 1961-1967: Claire Martin, "The New Song"; Monique Bosco, "My Loved Ones"; Suzanne de Padova, "The Contest Winner"; Laurent Girouard, "Mother's Day Won't Happen"; Denise Loiselle, "The Fiancée"; and Suzanne Martel, "Fille du Roy." No discussion of translation practice or theory.

548. Deraps, Danny. "L'Éleveur d'étalons: traduction en français de *The Studhorse Man*, de Robert Kroetsch." M.A. Université de Sherbrooke, Fall 1985.

Aucune discussion portant sur la théorie ou sur le processus de traduction.

549. Dion, Conrad. "Translation into English of Albert Laberge's *La Scouine*, with Critical Introduction." M.A. Université de Sherbrooke, 1973.

Claims that the translation stays as close to the original as possible, that he has not intended "to improve on the original or to correct possible faults, but rather to create a fair and exact representation of Laberge's novel"; outlines a few of the difficulties encountered, such as parallelism, synonymous adjectives, and abundance of relative pronouns in source text, and his solutions.

550. Duval, Jean. "Vaine illusion: traduction en français de *More Joy in Heaven* de Morley Callaghan." M.A. Université de Sherbrooke, 1973.

Aucune discussion portant sur la théorie ou sur le processus de traduction.

551. Fournier, Camille. "Traduction de *the sun is axeman* de Douglas G. Jones." M. Trad. Université de Montréal, 1978.

Parle des raisons qu'il avait de traduire Jones, de son désir de respecter le texte d'origine et de ses efforts pour reproduire l'essence des images et du style de Jones.

552. Goyette-Laberge, Suzanne. "Étude sur la traduction de quelques adjectifs (français-anglais)." M.A. Université de Montréal, 1973.

Étudie la traduction des adjectifs français rendus soit par un adjectif anglais correspondant soit par d'autres termes précis; parmi les exemples, on trouve *Agaguk* d'Yves Thériault (trad. Miriam Chapin) et *Alexandre Chenevert* de Gabrielle Roy (*The Cashier*, trad. Harry Lorin Binsse).

553. Guertin, Suzanne. "Irving Layton, de l'anglais au français." M.A. Université de Montréal, 1974.

Traduction de l'avant-propos de *The Swinging Flesh* et d'une trentaine de poèmes tirés de *Selected Poems* (1945-1960); traite en détail des problèmes et des solutions pour trouver des tournures équivalentes aux images colorées, à la syntaxe et à la grammaire de Layton présentes dans sa prose et sa poésie; commente le problème supplémentaire du rythme en poésie; se réfère aux catégories "mot image/mot signe" de la *Stylistique comparée du français et de l'anglais*. Avec commentaires et annotations.

554. Larkin, Catherine-Anne. "Traduction anglaise annotée de deux lettres de Marie de l'Incarnation. Étude de stylistique comparée." M.A. Université Laval, 1968.

Au moyen de la *Stylistique comparée du français et de l'anglais*, explique les difficultés rencontrées dans le passage du français à l'anglais et fait une description méthodique des procédés et des cadres de la stylistique comparée, qui servaient d'outils de traduction. S'attache aux problèmes concernant la traduction des archaïsmes et le vocabulaire mystique.

555. Lebel, Marc. "Traduction d'*Élégies civiles et autres poèmes* de Dennis Lee." M.A. Université de Sherbrooke, 1977.

L'introduction donne des renseignements sur la biographie de Lee et traite des théories et du style de ses poèmes; conclut avec des "Notes de l'auteur et du traducteur."

556. Macaulay, Barbara Constance. *Étude critique de la traduction de quatre textes publicitaires*. M.A. University of New Brunswick, 1982.

Analyse portant sur quatre traductions anglaises et françaises, dont un résumé de *La Sagouine* d'Antonine Maillet, basée sur l'évaluation de la qualité de la traduction qui est illustrée par la suite par des exemples d'erreurs, classées selon des catégories établies dans la *Stylistique comparée du français et de l'anglais*.

557. MacKay, Barbara Airdrie (Tennant). "A Translation of Marie-Claire Blais's *L'Insoumise*." M.A. University of New Brunswick, 1973.

Explains her process in translating Blais's novel (a literal draft followed by a more idiomatic version), and the lexical and stylistic problems encountered, including how and whether to translate grammatical flaws.

558. Macri, Francis M. "*Le Torrent* by Anne Hébert: A Translation and Commentary." M.A. University of Alberta, 1970.

Includes a history of translation theory and methods; discusses significance of a study of translation for the comparatist; explains problems and difficulties in translating Hébert's difficult style: *faux amis*, symbols and images, tone, dialogue, colloquialisms, onomatopoeia; gives detailed examples and justifies solutions.

559. Mezei, Kathy. "Anne Hébert, *Les Chambres de bois*: A Translation and Interpretation." M.A. Carleton University, 1971.

Introduction includes a chapter on "Language," describing the process of this translation of Hébert's novel, the appropriateness of literal translation, the danger of *faux amis*, the differences between French and English, and the difficulties created by Hébert's poetic, elliptical style.

560. Mickelson, Linda. "*Les Muets* (Albert Camus) et *Angoisse-de-Dieu* (Yves Thériault): étude commentée de la traduction anglaise." M.A. Université Laval, 1968.

Comparaison des textes originaux, des traductions et des traductions proposées, selon le modèle de la *Stylistique comparée du français et de l'anglais*, ce qui révèle les erreurs stylistiques et grammaticales importantes présentes dans la traduction du texte de Thériault.

561. Murray, Michael M. "Étude stylistique comparée de l'anglais et du français dans *Barometer Rising* et sa traduction *Le Temps tournera au beau*." M.A. Université Laval, 1967.

Utilisant des passages représentatifs de la description, des dialogues et de la narration, ainsi que des classifications établies dans la

Stylistique comparée du français et de l'anglais, Murray traite d'abord des réussites de Simard puis des erreurs lexicales et des erreurs au niveau du message.

562. Plourde, Marc. "A Translation of Gaston Miron's Poetry and Prose, with a Critical Introduction." M.A. Université de Montréal, 1980.

His chapter, "On Translating Miron," is published with only very minor changes in *Embers and Earth* and *The Insecurity of Art* [see 252].

563. Ravel, Aviva. "Contemporary Québécois Drama in Translation." M.A. Université de Montréal, 1976.

Thesis includes translations of Félix Leclerc, *L'Affaire décourageante*; Françoise Loranger, *Jour après jour*; Marcel Dubé, *De l'autre côté du mur*; Jacques Languirand, *Les Cloisons*; Robert Gurik, *63*; Michel Garneau, *Strauss et Pesant*; André Simard, *Le Temps d'une pêche*. Outlines method of translating: "a synthetic as opposed to an analytic procedure"; outlines specific concerns in translating drama; prefaces each translation with a brief discussion of problems and choices, in relation to *joual*, dialect, speech, cultural and linguistic context.

564. Rivière-Anderson, Christine. "Traduction de l'anglais au français de 'The Latehomecomer' et 'Baum, Gabriel 1935-( )' de Mavis Gallant." M.A. Université de Sherbrooke, 1983.

Briefly describes author, content, and style of two stories; outlines difficulties translating tense sequences and the title "The Latehomecomer."

565. Saint-Pierre, Yves. "Traduction de *La Nouvelle Inquisition* de Paul Toupin." M.A. Université de Sherbrooke, 1983.

Aucune discussion portant sur la théorie ou sur le processus de traduction.

566. Scott, Howard. "Louky Bersianik's *L'Euguélionne*: Problems of Translating the Critique of Language in New Quebec Feminist Writing." M.A. Concordia University, 1984.

Includes translation of selected passages of *L'Euguélionne*, and a theoretical discussion of problems encountered in the translation, raised by questions of gender and language.

567. Shouldice, Larry [Mason]. "Contemporary Quebec Criticism." Ph.D. Université de Montréal, 1978 [see 260].

568. Shouldice, Larry. "*Contes anglais et autres* de Jacques Ferron: introduction critique et traduction en anglais." M.A. Université de Sherbrooke, 1971.

    No discussion of translation practice or theory.

569. Sinave, André. "La Mort va mieux avec Coca-Cola: A Translation of Dave Godfrey, *Death Goes Better with Coca-Cola*." M.A. Université de Sherbrooke, 1970.

    Aucune discussion portant sur la théorie ou sur le processus de traduction.

570. Smith, Diane Lee. "Claire Martin in English: Theory and Practice of Literary Translation." M.A. University of Alberta, 1976.

    Translation of *Avec ou sans amour*; in her chapter, "Translating Claire Martin," Smith discusses minor problems with respect to historical or national differences between English Canada and Quebec, and difficulties caused by the short-story genre, style, linguistic comparison between French and English, *faux amis*, syntax, and dialogue.

571. Sotiropoulou-Papaleonidas, Irène. "Jacques Brault: théorie/pratique de la traduction: nouvelle approche de la problématique de la traduction poétique." M.A. Université de Sherbrooke, 1981 [voir 180].

572. Spiridonakis, Annette. "Problèmes de la traduction française d'une œuvre canadienne d'expression anglaise (les romans de Hugh MacLennan)." Ph.D. Université de Paris X, 1975.

    Classe et analyse les "écarts" commis par Louise Gareau Des Bois et Jean Simard dans leur traduction des romans de Hugh MacLennan. Compare les deux traducteurs.

573. Stockton, Julie May. "The Flowering Suns." M.A. York University, 1984.

    A translation of Jacques Ferron's *Les Grands Soleils*; states in Abstract that the problem is in creating "a workable stage play for an anglophone audience, while sustaining the uniquely French-Canadian flavour." Includes "Translator's Notes" which explain the "more obscure images" and the fashion in which they have been translated. Translation is taken from the second edition and is not an adaptation.

574. Stowe, John Stewart. "A Race Which Refuses to Die: une nouvelle traduction du roman *Menaud, maître-draveur* de Félix-Antoine Savard." M.A. University of New Brunswick, 1975.

Claims that Alan Sullivan's translation, *Boss of the River* (1947), contains "numerous incongruities of expression and style, with significant misinterpretations of the original text, and even totally incomprehensible passages in English"; using *Stylistique comparée du français et de l'anglais*, Stowe explains the inconsistencies in Sullivan. His own translation is "an attempt to render the author's original intentions and style as faithfully as possible, while respecting the limitations and differences between the two languages and cultures." Introduction includes a detailed discussion of Sullivan's errors in *spoken* language, *idiomatic* language, *figurative* language, and of his *faux amis*.

575. Tokatlian, Hamparsum. "Traduction de *Pleure pas, Germaine*, œuvre de Claude Jasmin." M.A. Université de Montréal, 1978.

In "Translator's Preface," describes his method and choices concerning equivalence in expressions and religious invocations, the recreation of the source text's choppy syntax, the rendering of *joual* by Montreal working class idiom, maintaining the central character's speech habits, and retention of French expressions; concludes with an appendix in which specific choices and problems are outlined.

576. Wickett, Margaret. Traduction poétique du recueil *Petits poèmes presque en prose* par Jean Éthier-Blais. M. Trad. Université de Montréal, 1981.

Discusses reasons for and method in translating these "prosaic" poems; explains why she decided to forego rhyme in her English version; concludes with "Explanatory Notes," which point out specific problems and choices.

577.   Czarnecki, Mark. Translator's Notes. *Surrealism and Quebec Literature: History of a Cultural Revolution*. By André G. Bourassa. Trans. Mark Czarnecki. Toronto: University of Toronto Press, 1984. 267-273.

Detailed translator's notes as end notes.

578.   Ellenwood, [William] Ray. Translator's Notes. *The Cart*. By Jacques Ferron. Trans. Ray Ellenwood. Toronto: Exile Editions, 1980. 139-144.

Includes a number of notes explicating references in the text and allusions to Ferron's other works; explains some of the Ferronesque and specifically French-Canadian terms used.

579.   Scully, Robert Guy. Translator's Notes. *Wild to Mild*. By Réjean Ducharme. Trans. Robert Guy Scully. Bilingual Edition. Saint-Lambert: Les Éditions Héritage, 1980.

Extensive translator's notes throughout the text; asterisk denotes words or expressions in English in the original.

580. Gagnon, André. "Translations of Children's Books in Canada." *Canadian Children's Literature* 45 (1987): 14-53.

Outlines the publishing history of translations of children's books, French to English, English to French, 1900 to present (1986). Notes that translations from English to French "outnumber those in the reverse direction by three to one." Points out examples of simultaneous translations, translations into French by Quebec publishers, and into English by English publishers, and bilingual books. Suggests authors who should be translated and that an annotated list of books to be translated be compiled annually.

581. Smiley, Barbara. "Canadian Children's Books in Translation— English and French." *In Review* 14 (February 1980): 14-20.

Includes three lists headed Translations from English to French (TE), Translations from French to English (TF), Bilingual Books (BB), and a title index which records titles published in both languages.

Author Index/Index des auteurs

This index is alphabetized letter by letter. In addition to authors, it includes all editors and compilers cited in this text. Reference to citations **about** authors are in italics, and those **by** authors are in roman script. All references to translators are in the translator index. Authors not listed in annotations, but referred to in article or review may be included.

Cet index est classé par ordre alphabétique et comprend aussi le nom des éditeurs et rédacteurs cités dans cet ouvrage. Les références **à propos** de citations d'auteurs sont imprimées en italique, celles faites **par** les auteurs sont en romain. On peut y trouver des auteurs cités dans des articles ou des critiques mais non dans leurs annotations.

Translator Index/
Index des traducteurs

This index is alphabetized letter by letter. Translators not listed in annotations, but referred to in article or review may be included.

Cet index est classé par ordre alphabétique. On peut y trouver des traducteurs cités dans des articles ou des critiques mais non dans leurs annotations.

Title Index/Index des titres

This index is alphabetized letter by letter. Journals and titles of articles are not included. Titles not listed in annotations, but referred to in article or review may be included. Titles of translations listed but not evaluated are not included.

Cet index, classé par ordre alphabétique, ne comprend pas les revues et les titres d'articles, ni les titres de traductions mentionnées mais non évaluées. On peut y trouver des titres cités dans des articles ou des critiques mais non dans leurs annotations.

Subject Index

This index is alphabetized letter by letter under the categories pertaining to literary translation. Note that there are two subject indexes—French and English. The English subject index indexes only items in English, while the French index indexes only items in French. A user who wishes a complete listing of items in both languages on, for example, literal translation, must look in the English subject index under "literal translation" and in the French subject index under "traduction littérale."

act of: 54
adaptation: 197, 299, 384
adaptation, dramatic: 142, 185, 188, 193, 194, 289, 302, 325, 376, 455, 493, 495, 517, 563
ambiguity: 300, 363, 439
art of: 51, 75, 109, 150, 288, 385, 498
author-translator relationship: 88, 93, 128, 132, 134, 176, 204, 207, 229, 241, 243, 258, 267, 270, 300, 398, 505

betrayal, translation as: see treason, translation as

Canada Council, policies of: 7, 33, 34, 121, 130, 131, 301, 381, 487
colloquialisms (see also dialect, *joual*): 37, 128, 185, 193, 194, 200, 203, 218, 220, 244, 250, 253, 282, 290, 298, 299, 300, 301, 308, 326, 334, 350, 354, 371, 376, 396, 417, 418, 420, 446, 447, 453, 464, 492, 510, 514, 540, 558, 578
comparatist, translator as: 120, 262, 263, 285, 558

comparison of translation activity in Quebec and English Canada: see situation
comparison of translation and creative writing: 13, 28, 97, 134, 144, 202, 256, 258, 307, 375, 422, 529, 533
criticism, translation as: 41, 361
cultural context: 5, 7, 8, 9, 13, 29, 35, 37, 38, 51, 58, 61, 67, 69, 70, 71, 77, 80, 96, 100, 104, 112, 113, 114, 118, 119, 120, 121, 185, 186, 207, 216, 232, 240, 256, 258, 268, 283, 288, 290, 304, 306, 337, 361, 416, 422, 426, 475, 527, 563, 570, 578
cultural difference: 8, 59, 112, 496
cultural myths generated by translation: 51, 288
cultural role: 5, 7, 9, 20, 33, 35, 38, 49, 51, 80, 96, 100, 109, 113, 114, 118, 119, 121, 127, 129, 130, 138, 140, 198, 232, 236, 255, 256, 278, 280, 288, 293, 297, 299, 305, 315, 330, 333, 381, 457, 502
cultural transposition: 472

dialect (see also colloquialisms, *joual*): 32, 67, 85, 104, 128, 193, 200,

Index des sujets

Cet index est classé par ordre alphabétique et par catégories propres à la traduction littéraire. Il existe deux index de sujets, un en anglais, l'autre en français, chacun n'indiquant que les sujets traités dans cette langue; ainsi, pour obtenir, par exemple, toutes les informations se rapportant à la "traduction littérale," il faudra chercher sous "literal translation" les renseignements complémentaires anglais.

Achevé d`imprimer
en mai 1988 sur les presses
des Ateliers Graphiques Marc Veilleux Inc.
Cap-Saint-Ignace, Qué.